Learning Curves

LIFE LESSONS LEARNED WHILE RIDING A HARLEY DAVIDSON MOTORCYCLE

Roy A. Hammond and Douglas R. Andrew

Also by Douglas R. Andrew

BEST-SELLERS:

Missed Fortune

Missed Fortune 101

The Last Chance Millionaire

Millionaire By Thirty

Baby Boomer Blunders

Create Your Own Economic Stimulus

How to Have LASER Focus

Published 2015
by Live Abundant Publications
Salt Lake City, Utah U.S.A.
Printed in U.S.A.

ISBN: 978-0-9740087-2-1

Any mention of vehicle manufacturers or authors/speakers within *Learning Curves* does not imply endorsement of this book, its authors, publisher or related foundations.

ACKNOWLEDGMENTS

An author's work can be unique only in the expression of ideas, which rarely, if ever, claim just one originator. Ideas are the result of countless interactions with people who influence the path one takes.

We wish to express sincere gratitude for the wonderful people who have helped and inspired us to create *Learning Curves.*

We each offer gratitude to our wives. Roy is grateful to Frances, his first wife of 48 years, for her incredible support and love. Frances passed away in 2009 and Roy remarried Glenda (Doug's sister), who lost her husband of 46 years, Gary, to cancer. Roy is very thankful for Glenda who continues by his side in life and his Learning Curves endeavors. Doug is grateful for his wife and companion of 40 years, Sharee, who has been by his side rendering assistance and encouragement with every project he has undertaken. We love you wonderful women dearly for your support and encouragement!

Roy and Doug are grateful for each other and the incredible working relationship they have by combining their unique abilities and passion for life while serving others. May we continue to ride Harleys into the sunset of life with an undying passion to add to our book of "I Remember When" memories and lessons learned while riding together.

To our families and friends we offer gratitude for the blessings of life and wonderful support you all give us. Our greatest joy comes from being together as we continue to have a lifetime learning commitment. Doug is grateful for his brother, Sherm, his first motorcycle buddy, who was taken tragically in an accident in 1999.

We are grateful and express appreciation to Heather Beers, our wonderful friend and editor. We sincerely appreciate her special talents and encouragement. We extend special thanks to Toni Lock at tmdesigns for her expertise in the layout of this work. And we express thanks to Jolene Farley for her unique and professional artwork and illustrations.

We appreciate the many teachers and mentors in our lives. Special thanks to Dan Sullivan, Joe Polish, Robert Cooper, Marshall Thurber, Lee Brower, Richard Rossi and Leo Weidner for your encouragement, inspiration, tools and advice.

And thank you to the awesome team of people and volunteers who work with both of us in our professional and philanthropic endeavors. TEAM truly means **T**ogether **E**veryone **A**chieves **M**ore. Together we are better—and we can turn this world right side up!

TABLE OF CONTENTS

INTRODUCTION

Unquestionably, Roy A. Hammond and Douglas R. Andrew are motorcycle enthusiasts. This book is about far more than actual–real-life experiences they have had while riding Harley Davidson motorcycles. Roy, now in his early 70s, and Doug, now in his early 60s, have experienced a plethora of challenges and victories physically, socially, emotionally, spiritually, financially—yes in every dimension of their lives. Their long "learning curves" of life have helped them gain insights to abundant living—how to overcome setbacks in life and make the learning greater than the experience. Their hope for you, the reader, is to empower you so you will experience a much shorter "power curve" of learning than maybe what they went through to learn some of life's greatest lessons. They invite you along for the ride as they talk from their hearts about what they have learned; so please listen with your heart more than your ears to their messages. They want you to "feel" the meaning behind the story and the principles that they teach. Their goal is to create a meaningful transformation in your life as they share true principles, teach proven strategies and concepts and also disclose some of the best tools they have employed to accomplish an abundant life. This book purposely isn't information-based. Be prepared for an insight-based experience as you read and get epiphanies on opportunities that maybe you didn't know existed.

Roy is a world-renowned retired dentist who now is passionate about philanthropic service to people in third-world countries who need a hand-up—not a hand out. These people "earn" the right to receive dental work and care from the 50 or so dental professionals that Roy recruits as volunteers for every trip he sponsors with his foundation, Smiles for Hope—which supports a larger foundation, Smiles for Life. Please go to **www.LearningCurvesBook.com** for more information. Roy began his humanitarian efforts more than 25 years ago when he and his wife Frances made their first trip to Micronesia in 1987. Roy experienced the real world of the less fortunate of developing countries. From that beginning he and his wife started their own Private Foundation and began their journey. Roy has now hosted over 100 groups to several countries in Africa and to Nepal and Vietnam, Mexico, Bolivia, Peru,

Guatemala and the Dominican Republic. Roy and his wife, Glenda, have also built a small hospital in Nepal that provides dental care and emergency medical care to over 300,000 people who previously had no access to care.

Roy began Learning Curves as a means to help fund his charitable work in third-world countries. Learning Curves tours are organized Harley Davidson motorcycle adventures to some of the most incredible sites in America and the world and involve continuing education as the core of the tour. Learning Curves started out as continuing education experience for dentists. It now has expanded to include all kinds of professionals who love riding motorcycles and want to hob-nob and learn from some of the best entrepreneurial minds on the planet. Please go to **www.LearningCurvesBook.com** for more information.

Roy and his first wife of 48 years, Frances, began this journey together in 1987. Frances passed away in 2009. Subsequently, Roy met his second wife, Glenda (Doug's sister) in 2010 and they were married shortly thereafter and have continued a commitment to their charitable causes together. Glenda had lost her first husband of 46 years, Gary, to pancreatic cancer. They are so fortunate to have found each other and enjoy a rich life serving others.

More than 40 years ago, Doug Andrew established his own financial services practice and quickly established a reputation as a trusted financial strategist. A few years later, Doug and his wife, Sharee, experienced a "defining moment," an unexpected financial setback that changed the way they not only handled their own finances, but also the advice Doug gave to his clients. He adamantly refused to "follow the crowd" and instead delved into extensive research to develop his unique and powerful financial philosophy of liquidity, safety, and rate of return.

In an effort to share his experiences and lessons learned to a broader audience, he wrote his original book, *Missed Fortune.* Doug was thrust on the national stage with the *Missed Fortune* book series that followed, including *Missed Fortune 101* (business best-seller), *The Last Chance Millionaire* (New York Times best-seller and Wall Street Journal #1), and *Millionaire by Thirty* (written with his two sons Emron and Aaron). He is a national radio host and has appeared on PBS, Fox Business, and CBS. He is also a nationally sought-after speaker and has presented for organizations such as Tony Robbins and the Asset Protection Group.

Today he is surrounded by a team of expert financial strategists, Wealth Architects who join Doug in his mission to help clients live an abundant life. They have helped thousands of people not only prepare for and live a prosperous retirement, but also to focus on all aspects of Authentic Wealth—foundational, intellectual and financial assets.

And for Doug, who is as passionate about his family as he is helping others realize their abundant potential, life couldn't be better. Doug and Sharee love to spend time together—date nights, lunch a couple days a week, weekend getaways, trips to Hawaii or New Zealand and even exercising. They also love being with their children and grandchildren. They all get together regularly; they have Family Vacations with a Purpose; and they even have Grandpa's Treehouse (a luxury treehouse with air conditioning, swings, and nonstop fun).

Doug shares many of their experiences in this book—which makes the book all the more meaningful for him. He has been thrilled to co-author this book with his brother-in-law, Dr. Roy Hammond and share yet another dimension of his life with the world. For more background on Doug and his work helping others achieve Authentic Wealth, visit **www.LearningCurvesBook.com**.

1 IT'S NOT ABOUT THE DESTINATION IT'S THE JOURNEY

Roy:

When I was growing up and we would take family vacations, it didn't matter where we were going—Yellowstone National Park, Fish Lake, Mt. Rushmore, or to see my Uncle Clyde up north on the Canadian Border—it seems like I spent all my time concerned about when we were going to get there.

I recall peppering my mom and dad with questions like, "How much longer?" or "Are we almost there?" As I look back now, I realize how my constant concern about getting the journey over with must have been a serious interruption to their enjoyment of the journey.

But now in adulthood, I see it all differently. When my wife and I pack up the Harley and head out, we often have no destination in mind, and if we do we look for the longest distance possible to get there. We are always looking for the "road less traveled." We want to take a new route, and we even take dead-end side roads just to see what's there.

GET IT DONE ... OR SOAK IT IN?

It seems that in today's world, too many of us approach life like I did my family's road trips when I was young. We box ourselves into an automobile or a plane and then take the quickest highway or airline route to our destination. We focus so much on "getting there, doing the vacation thing, then getting home" that we miss out on much of the adventure.

I believe that the anticipation is at least half of the joy of any event in our lives. If we over-expedite the whole experience, we have deprived ourselves.

Think about it—are we approaching life just like our "get it done" trips? It seems to me that without conscious awareness, life can take on the same urgency. We rush to the next phase of life, always imagining that elusive happiness is just around the corner.

But what if instead we slowed the pace and found joy in each mile? I have always felt that the true purpose of life is to grow stronger. So like riding, as we conquer life's steep inclines, bask in the straight stretches surrounded by beautiful forests and snow-capped mountains, and get ready for the sharp uphill hairpin curves, we're learning, growing, and taking it all in. Even the added smell of fresh cut alfalfa, or the scent of a recent rain storm (or the foul stench of a road-kill skunk!) brings a dimension to the journey that cannot be duplicated and should be enjoyed.

THE BUMPS ALONG THE WAY

When we sit around the table and talk about the memories of our past rides, we don't remember the ones where there were no challenges or unexpected paths. We tend to remember the setbacks, the bumps, the falls, the difficult turns and the mountains we climbed.

Just the same, when we sit on the front porch of life surrounded by our grandchildren, it won't be those times when we were never challenged that we recount. Our thoughts will go to the tough, harrowing, exciting times. We'll point out these opportunities that we were given by our Creator to grow stronger, to become wiser, and to have more compassion.

ENJOYING THE EDUCATION

As I look back and consider my own life experiences, I think I've benefited most from making a plan (and enjoying the planning), working the plan (and enjoying the working), and then completing the plan (and enjoying the results).

I have vivid memories of my educational journey. Being married at a very young age ... and with three years of college and four years of dental school still ahead, it would have been easy to say, "We just have to gut through it, and we will finally be happy after dental school graduation." But my wife and I made a conscious emotional AND verbal decision to enjoy the journey. With our slim budget and minimal free time, we set out on our journey with an eye towards creative use of our time and financial resources. We decided early on to make the most of this opportunity, to plan and grow and learn and enjoy the process.

We made lifelong friendships along the way. Some of my fondest memories are those of my wife and I being out on our own, solving the challenges that came our way. We created ideas for saving money and managing our budget. In our kitchen cupboard we had several baby food jars. Each jar was labeled with a particular section of our budget. When the paycheck would come each month, it was turned into cash, and a certain amount of the cash went into each jar. We were able to visually monitor the use of our resources for both saving and having fun. The budget became a game as we kept score year after year.

Rather than running from the stern and difficult professors at my dental school, we were open to building relationships. The assistant dean eventually asked us regularly to stay the weekend with his children while he and his wife traveled. One of the doctors, the meanest of the mean clinic professors, invited a few of our class members to go to his private dental office where he could teach us a few of his personal tricks.

We loved and enjoyed the city and the state where we lived and worked during those years. Graduation was bittersweet, because it meant leaving behind the joy of this part of our life's journey.

ENJOYING EACH PHASE

We then began a new leg of our journey in starting a new business. It would have again been easy to think, "This is so hard … we won't be happy until we are successful." But once again, we emotionally and verbally committed that we would enjoy the journey. And as we looked back at those early years with the practice, they were just as joyful.

It's been like that all along, as we've learned life becomes a journey of commitments to enjoy. Man is that he might have joy, but "if it's going to be, it's up to me." My commitment now is to endure to the end with joy in the journey. For me in my life, this takes a constant renewal of planning, working, and enjoying it all each step of the path.

I reiterate … there is no destination in life, only a journey. I believe our purpose here is to prepare us for continued joy and love in this life and the next. I want to commit myself each day to adding wisdom to my knowledge by making the most of every steep incline, every hairpin turn and bump in the road. I invite you to enjoy the ride, right along with me!

Doug's Take:

MY FIRST MOTORCYCLE

Sharee, my wife, and I married in February of 1974. We were both in school, going after our degrees. I worked at Kentucky Fried Chicken and Sharee worked at a bookstore. Within 90 days of our wedding, I purchased my first motorcycle. It was a four-stroke Honda 125. I remember riding it home from the dealership on a back road because I did not yet have my motorcycle endorsement from the driver's license division. Sure enough, a police car was taking radar in the neighborhood, and I was going 35 mph in a 25 mph zone.

The patrolman pulled me over to issue me a speeding ticket. He then discovered that I did not have a motorcycle endorsement and issued me another ticket. He then asked for my inspection certificate and temporary license tag. The dealership had neglected to put it on my bike. So the officer wrote me third ticket. He said I would have to walk the motorcycle home. I told him I had to be to work at KFC within 30 minutes, so he obliged following me to our apartment about a mile away. Sharee had our car at the bookstore, and I could not find a ride.

So, I took the risk and sneaked out of our apartment the back way and headed to work on my motorcycle. The first four-way stop I came to, a police car approached on my right. My heart dropped to my stomach! Fortunately it was a different officer. I waved and smiled. He waved back and I was on my way to work on time. Needless to say, the next day I immediately went in, got my motorcycle endorsement and picked up my license plate. That was the beginning of my motorcycling journey.

THE BIKE AFFAIR CONTINUES

A year later, my brother Sherm and I purchased Yamaha Enduro 250 dirt bikes, and we rode whenever we could find the time in the foothills above Utah Valley. We even sometimes went riding at 2 am, because it was the only time we could squeeze it in amid our busy lives. It was never really about arriving at a destination; it was about the experience of the ride.

I didn't get my first Harley until 1999. There were waiting lists of one to two years to get a Harley at the time, which made it all the more sweet. It was a metallic midnight blue and silver ice Road King Classic. I'll talk more about my experiences on a Harley in future chapters.

ROUGH ROAD AHEAD

I am also a serious "Jeeper." I have a Jeep Rubicon that will climb a tree. It is well-equipped for the rugged adventures we go on. Yes, I have been on all of the most difficult trails in Moab, Utah—several times. It's always the experiences along the trails that we reminisce about. Every July, our family takes our Jeep, ATVs and dirt bikes, and we journey to a special lake in the Wind River Range of Wyoming (southeast of Yellowstone Park). The terrain is extremely rugged. The journey to get to our campsite from Salt Lake City takes 12 hours.

When we finally arrive, the setting is spectacular at 9,500 feet above sea level, and the fishing is fantastic. But the journey in and out is as much or more of the experience than the destination. It takes three hours just to navigate the final 12 miles as we creep and crawl over boulders that would destroy any stock four-wheel drive vehicle. Sometimes, when we take guests in, they seem anxious as they keep asking, "When are we going to get there?" I'm having to constantly remind them that the journey in and out is more the unique experience than the actual destination.

So it is with life. It's overcoming each and every obstacle that makes you feel you are progressing into rarely traveled terrain. And the rewards as we conquer the challenges are unbelievingly satisfying. As we have a new experience every year—we reach a bend, a rock slide, a set of boulders, a newly fallen tree—we reflect on all the times we encountered similar challenges. We recall how we winched our way out, turned our vehicle upright, fixed the problem, and we feel prepared to rack up another learning experience to add to life's wonderful memories.

MAKE THE ENJOYMENT GREATER THAN THE EFFORT

In my professional and personal life, I have seen similar lessons apply in countless ways. I'll share a few of these experiences gleaned along the way.

As a financial strategist and retirement planning specialist for more than 40 years, I have developed an entrepreneurial attitude and subsequently started several businesses. As a result, I have coached many successful business owners. The fact is all of us are involved in the "busy-ness" of life.

A wonderful entrepreneurial coach and dear friend, Dan Sullivan, released a book a few years ago that became an Amazon number one best-seller. It was titled, *10 Laws of Lifetime Growth.* A few of his students helped contribute to some of the laws outlined in that wonderful book. One of the laws states that you should always make your enjoyment greater than your effort.

This has been a difficult thing for me to learn in my life, primarily because I'm a perfectionist. Everything has always had to be perfect. When we entertained people or had friends over for dinner or held a wedding banquet or other function, everything always had to be just right. I was running around making sure that things were in order. If we had inclement weather, it stressed me out. Finally I came to realize I was the only one NOT enjoying the occasion. I saw that my friends, associates and guests had really come for the interaction and wanted my attention. They wanted to mingle. They did not care if there was a piece of lint on the carpet or dust or fingerprints on the piano. What they wanted was me to enjoy the occasion with them.

Of course this doesn't apply only to getting ready for dinner parties. If we can make our enjoyment greater than our effort with our professions, with our families, with our friends, and even with our setbacks in life, we will truly have lived.

Since learning this, I have always strived to make the enjoyment in any activity, project or event, much greater than the effort. This has helped me live a more stress-free life and enjoy family, friends and relationships.

MAKE YOUR LEARNING GREATER THAN YOUR EXPERIENCE

In his book, Mr. Sullivan also recommended making your learning greater than the experience. Whether it's a good experience or a bad one, there's something greater that can be learned—and shared—from the significant moments in our lives.

I'm an instructor and speaker for an organization known as the Asset Protection Foundation. This organization is one of the top in the country for helping people who have spent their lifetime accumulating assets, but have yet not protected them. The goal is to help people guard their assets from frivolous lawsuits through firewalls of protection, such as corporations or limited liability companies, or LLCs.

In our family, we have a different definition of LLC. It stands for Lifetime Learning Commitment, and it provides somewhat similar protection, but for us it's from life's setbacks. We have strived to teach our children and grandchildren to always learn and have a never-ending lifetime of making all experiences contribute to greater learning. Therefore, whenever we have any experience, be it good or bad (it could be a vacation, a meeting, a family reunion or even a marriage), we simply go through a process in order to learn and transform that experience for the next time we have a similar experience.

I have kept the same basic process Dan Sullivan teaches:

- We write down the experience that we want to learn from and improve.
- Then we list the things that worked.
- We list on the other side the things that didn't work or that went wrong.
- Then we write down (if we were going to have a similar experience like this again), what we would do differently the next time to have a better outcome.
- Finally, we write down a step-by-step process about what we would do first, second, third, fourth and so on, in order to pull off a much better result the next go-around.

This has helped our family immensely to make the learning greater than the experience. In Chapter 3, I will illustrate some of the actual ways that we have made our learning greater than our experience.

I REMEMBER WHEN

As we go through life, whether it's at work or home, with friends or extended family, we all have unique experiences. Some are uplifting, others are defining, and some are just plain funny. But what often happens? Life keeps zipping by and these great moments slip to the back of our minds. They might become fuzzy, or we might forget them altogether. But what if we kept them fresh, shared them, and they could keep giving their energy and insight for years to come? This is something we've done with our employees and our children and grandchildren. It's called "I Remember When," and it has made all the difference in how we have grown closer, preserved precious memories and, really, just had a blast together. I got the idea from a good friend, Lee Brower.

One of the great traditions that we have conducted in our family is Family Vacations with a Purpose. These are getaways that can be as simple as a night or two away at a family cabin or nearby hotel, or as extravagant as a tropical week at a lush resort. Wherever you go, it's important to plan a mix of activities that are purposeful, bonding, inspiring and fun.

Our family has a Family Vacation with a Purpose every six months. Some of these vacations are as simple as a camping trip up the canyon or even a conversation in the basement of our home. Every other year we meet in Maui, Hawaii. We have been doing this for over 20 years.

Now some people hear this and they want to be a member of our family for a free trip to Maui. I didn't say it was free. In fact, ever since our children were teenagers they knew two years in advance on the odd years that we were going to meet in February for our retreat. They needed to schedule time off work, off school, without missing grades and arrange for themselves to be there because we don't want any empty chairs on our family vacations.

We taught them how we can meet in places like Maui, Hawaii, almost as inexpensively as staying home. We have bought time shares for pennies on the dollar that helped people who were trying to liquidate them simply for the price of bringing their property taxes current. We have rented out half of the time shares, which paid for the maintenance fees on ours. Therefore the lodging can be essentially free.

Our children use credit cards responsibly and rack up enough air miles in two years that many times their airfare is free. We pool our money and go grocery shopping and fix many of the meals in the condos. This way we can meet in Maui, Hawaii, almost as inexpensively as at home.

One of our favorite activities (for our six children with spouses and 14 grandchildren) is every evening at dinner, every family comes with three I Remember When memories. Now that they are old enough we not only record these, but they come with them on a thumb drive, so we can add them to our family book of memories. This book gets larger and larger every time we have a family retreat! If you do the math, a family our size currently with 27 family members, times three memories means that we add over 80 new memories in our family book every family vacation.

These "I Remember When" memories must fit on one page, which is typically under 750 words and they must be a real-life memory. All too often in life, these are the kind of experiences that people talk about; they reminisce; they cry; they laugh; but they usually never write them down. Through this system you can begin to collect a record of all the incredible experiences that you have had.

MY OWN REMEMBER WHEN

When our family first started doing this, I came up with a list of 77 memories or defining moments in my life. I've added 40 or 50 since then, and our children absolutely love these moments. They seem to especially like the one about the night my father had me turn myself into the police (it's not what it sounds like, or maybe it is?).

Another favorite was when I talked about "When wisdom knocks, don't give it a busy signal." I had five different examples of how I was motivated to do something, and when wisdom knocked, I didn't turn away, I pursued the endeavor and it brought great blessings.

I've loved hearing my family talk about the value of hard work, or how they met their spouses. Of course there's the time we were at Disneyland and my son Emron was in line for the bobsleds doing tricks on the handrail—he fell and did a face plant in the petunias as we were ready to get on. The stories that are shared can be over-the-top incredible!

This activity has since extended from my own family and employees to now my siblings. In fact, we just recently held our first annual get-together up at our cabin. All the siblings and spouses brought three stories. We started sharing over dinner Sunday night, then kept the stories going over breakfast and even lunch the next day. There were 10 of us, so we ended up gathering 30 stories total. Imagine what that will be when we do this over five years—150 stories! It will be a book our children and grandchildren will treasure forever.

As Roy indicated it is usually the experiences where something went wrong that we are writing about. Those are the learning experiences that we like to remember.

LIBERATION FROM PERFECTIONISM

As indicated, I often would get hung up earlier in my life because I was a perfectionist. Dan Sullivan also helped cure me from perfectionism. It's interesting that many people strive to achieve the ideal. This is a good aspiration. The problem is many of us beat ourselves up because of how much we still fall short.

As a Christian, I taught the life of Christ for eight years at an Institute of Religion on a volunteer basis. In Matthew 5:48, the often-recited verse states, "Be ye therefore perfect." The Hebrew translation of that is, be ye therefore *becoming*. Which insinuates that it's not so much in the destination but in the journey. That it's a never-ending path of progress.

This epiphany helped me realize that it's really all about progress, not perfection. We look towards that high bar of perfection and often, just like when we are riding that motorcycle, we hit one mountain peak and we see the next mountain peak that we never saw before. As a pilot of a small plane, I fly towards the horizon. But it's interesting that the horizon constantly stays far out there. And just like with flight, sometimes we cannot land at our final destination until we have achieved certain other mid-points on the way. This is like the path to our ideal, abundant life.

When we constantly measure how far we're still lacking, we can get depressed or upset. It's what Dan Sullivan calls being in the "gap"—the gap between where we are now and where we still want to be. We really need to learn to measure backward. In other words, to take time to celebrate where we used be. Think of it in terms of pastimes or talents and it makes sense. With our ability to play a musical instrument or ride a motorcycle or run a business. As we take time to acknowledge where we used to be and where we are now, then we can objectively look towards the next step with confidence to achieve a better life ahead.

I'm convinced many women will absolutely waltz into heaven. But, often women will admit they're the biggest culprits of comparing themselves with others. There's Suzie, who always bakes bread and cookies when new neighbors move in. Or Joanie who gets up and exercises every day. Or Laura, who reads a book a week.

In actuality, most people are comparing themselves to others while those people are comparing themselves to you! Competition really comes from the root word competence. We should measure our competence against where we have been and where we are now. And then, we can look objectively to our competence increasing in the future rather than creating competition, comparing ourselves to others and how we may fall short. Let's take time to applaud our successes!

THE 80% APPROACH

Probably the most powerful tool that I learned from Mr. Sullivan is what he calls the 80% Approach. I was always waiting until everything was perfect before I moved forward. My first book that I published, which became a best-seller, took over 10 years to complete because I kept waiting for it to be perfect. It sat on my credenza in manuscript form for over three years doing nobody any good because it wasn't right yet.

I was liberated from this attitude when I began to realize that people simply wanted the information. They didn't care if it was perfect. So Dan taught me that when it was 80% there; just print it. Speak it. Teach it. Send it. Whatever project you are doing; when it is 80% done, simply do it. Then you will get feedback (if you ask) from people who benefited from you sharing. That feedback is often times much better than a dozen publisher editors looking at the manuscript.

When I finally printed 500 copies of my first book, I sold 420 of them in two days. I told every one of them that I would send them a final copy if they would please send me back any points that were not clear, or any typographical or grammatical errors that they noticed. I received all kinds of great feedback, and I tweaked the second edition 30 days later. By tweaking the second addition, which only had 20% remaining that needed to be perfected, I tweaked that to 80%. So my second addition went from 80% perfect to 96% perfect (which is 80% of the last 20%).

I received additional feedback from those readers because I printed 2,500 copies of the second edition. Then I took that feedback and tweaked the final 4% that wasn't perfect to 80%. For the third edition, we printed 5,000 copies and it was theoretically 99.2% perfect. This all happened in a period of 90 days. It was the fourth addition that I tweaked 80% of the last 0.8% that got the attention of Warner Business Books, the number one business book editor in the world at the time. And they purchased the rights to my book and offered me a $100,000 advance to write the next book. If I was still waiting for it to be perfect it, would still be on my credenza 12 years later, doing nobody any good.

If Sharee and I had waited until it was perfect to start having children we would still be childless today. Amid all kinds of challenges, we just started our family and now we are blessed with six children and 14 grandkids. We somehow made it.

If I wanted to go to a Utah Jazz basketball game and I called the chief of police and said, "Sir I want to go to the ball game tonight, the Jazz are playing the Miami Heat, but I'm not going to leave my house until all the lights are green..." he would think he was talking to some kind of a nut. If you get in motion and you start adding value; even if the first light is red, it shortly turns green and you will get to the ball game on time, 95% of the time. But you must get in motion and be adding value for that to happen.

GET OUT OF YOUR COMFORT ZONE!

As people embark on new beginnings, be it a New Year, a new business, a new life, a new you, it's likely that everyone feels at least a little of what I call PAIN, or Pushback Against Ideas that are New. Until we can help ourselves to consistently move past that PAIN, we'll keep ourselves from growth.

Why do we resist change so much? Why are we so bound and determined to hold to what we know, to stay within the proverbial comfort zone? I remember as a child I was talking with my mother when she asked, "What are you going to do for your science fair project, Doug?"

I replied with something like, "I think I'll do the one I did last year because I already have the posters made." She wisely asked, "Son are you always going to take the course of least resistance?"

Yes, actually, I was hoping to. But that sort of living leads us to meandering through life with the least amount of effort, getting less-than-optimal results. I never forgot that. In fact, I have since realized I have never grown in my life until I got out of my comfort zone. It's not until we make our confidence, or faith, greater than our comfort that we push ourselves into new realms of success.

As I look back, I remember the first time I ever spoke on the radio I was nervous. I was terrified the first time I talked to an audience of 100 people, then 1000 people, and then 5000 people. I didn't think I could handle the pressure the first time I stepped in front of a television camera or was interviewed on live TV. Sure you have those butterflies but you learn to tame them. And then with enough practice and improvement, what may have started out a little shaky can become some of your greatest strengths.

One of the criteria I've learned to look for when determining if I'm going to seize any new opportunity is: if it's going to cause me to stretch but it's still within my unique ability, I will seize that opportunity. Yes, I actually run toward the PAIN. Because I have discovered that when you get out of your comfort zone; that is where the magic happens.

This principle applies to everything in life. Have you ever learned a new language? It's terribly awkward at first, but with time what once sounded like complete jibberish becomes a beautiful way to connect with new people and express yourself. Or what about taking up a new sport? I'm one of those who used to cringe at the thought of daily exercise. I preferred to just be active with pastimes like skiing and racquetball. But in the past few years my wife, Sharee, and I have transformed our lives with better nutrition and consistent, focused exercise. We box, run, strength train — and it's brought about phenomenal changes to our health.

Getting past the comfort zone of what we know also applies to financial planning. I have advised literally thousands of people to stop following the crowd and adopt financial planning strategies that provide better safety, liquidity and rate of return. At first, people have often posed a little resistance — these strategies are not necessarily what they learned back in business class. But as they have taken the time to understand the principles and set things in motion, they have continued on to abundant lives that have blessed not only themselves, but also their families and favorite charities.

And now back to your personal goals. If you're meeting with that wave of discomfort that comes from stepping outside the comfort zone, help yourself see that the PAIN is worth pushing through. Set specific goals for getting past it, and then celebrate the improved results on the other side, where the magic starts happening.

In every aspect of life, remember that anytime you have opportunities that are within your unique ability, seize them. Always make your confidence greater than your comfort level, and you will look back and say, "Wow, I'm glad I stretched, look what I'm capable of now!" Enjoy the journey of new opportunities, new horizons, and even more abundance.

RETHINK YOUR THINKING

We usually relate the acronym UFO to "Unidentified Flying Objects." In this book we will pose three introspective questions at the end of each chapter to think about. The questions will reflect key principles covered in the chapter, as they relate to three distinct circles of influence in all of our lives:

"U" meaning how the principles relate to YOU

"F" meaning how you can empower FAMILY and FRIENDS to implement the ideas

"O" meaning how you can influence OTHERS with whom you work and serve in all capacities

U: ***How can YOU reassess your own life to …***

- *Enjoy the journey?*
- *Increase your learning?*
- *Capture memories?*
- *Liberate yourself from perfectionism?*
- *Get out of your comfort zone?*
- *Live life to the fullest?*

F: ***How can you help facilitate and empower your close circle of FAMILY and FRIENDS to do the same —to live abundantly and enjoy the journey of life better?***

O: ***How can you influence OTHERS with whom you work and serve to enjoy their journey of life more?***

2

YOU GO WHERE YOU LOOK

Roy:

As I think back over my years of riding, I think one of the most difficult lessons I have had to learn is that the bike will go where you look, no matter where you plan to go in your mind.

If you are headed down a straight stretch of road and begin to gaze too long at the beautiful scenery to your right, the bike will begin to drift to the right. The same is true if you focus for an extended time toward the left. As you enter a turn you must direct your eyes out of the turn as far as possible, to the point where you want the bike to carry you; if you look down at where you are, you are in trouble. If you look to the side of the road during the turns, you are in deep trouble. If you look at the oncoming car in the opposite lane, well, let's just say you are in even deeper trouble.

So how does this lesson relate to our ride through life? We can travel through life with good intentions, and in our own mind it is easy for us to feel that those intentions are our reality. If we believe we're doing good, we *are* good, right?

But those who love us and stand by us through thick and thin (and those who see us as mentors) do not live in the world of our intentions, they live in the world of what we actually *do*. Our good intentions are not reality for them, only our actions.

We may have meant to make a smooth, safe turn on our life's path, but we were distracted by dishonesty, ill temper, pride, disloyalty, and the list goes on. When we turn our life's focus to these ungodly distractions, our life will turn in an unwanted direction.

LOOKING "OVER THERE"

I remember growing up as the oldest son of my father. I always wanted to be just like him. My father was a family medical doctor. He was respected, soft spoken, reliable and always willing to do more than he was asked to do. I was in junior high school when I set my sights on my professional goals, and emulating my father's abilities. I decided to follow him into medical practice, and while he was a doctor, I chose to be a dentist. (I realized as I got older that the demands of his practice detracted from the time he was able to give to his role as a father and husband—a dental practice would allow more flexibility.)

About that same time in my life, I met a young woman in ninth grade who would later become my wife. She had the attributes that became my source of connection to spirituality and God. I benefited from her example for just under a year, as she moved out of the country at the end of that school year.

I changed to a different school and different friends. Not really understanding what I do now, I soon forgot to look where I had committed that I wanted to go in life. Through my high school years, I thought I could look at all kinds of distractions and still stay safely on the path I had intended.

I learned a lot of hard lessons during those three years. My father did all in his power to help those lessons become turning points, to help return my focus to the future I had outlined. I tried college directly after high school and failed terribly. After one quarter, I joined the military. After returning from my time in the military, my ninth-grade mentor reentered my life.

LOOKING AHEAD

I now had renewed purpose and commitment to "look where I wanted to go," and one-and-a-half years later we were married. That purpose and commitment has continued ever since. I was blessed that those distractions did not lead me into the oncoming lane for a head-on collision with a truck or bus. My distractions were such that I was able to make a correction as I rounded that hairpin curve of life in high school. For that I am most grateful.

The sad reality of life, however, is that there are many enticing distractions that we cannot correct from with ease. Some have longer, deeper consequences than others. It may be different for everyone, so the key is to consider what is a distraction for you: infidelity, alcohol, drugs, dishonesty?

You go where you look. If you look long enough in an unintended direction, it may be impossible to make a recovery and get back on the path. As I said in the beginning of this chapter, this has been one of the most difficult riding lessons I have had to learn. It is also one of the most difficult life's lessons I have had to learn. My hope now is that I can continue to remember this principle as those inviting distractions come into view along my path in this life.

Because I feel it echoes the message of this chapter, I want to share a parable I wrote some time back.

THE PARABLE OF SPOT

When I observe unusual situations, I have a DNA-need to apply these situations to the principles of our daily lives.

One spring day, my wife, Glenda, and I were at Zion National Park making some arrangements for our Grand Circle ride in September through this beautiful area.

We spent the night at Zion Mountain Ranch. It is a huge cattle ranch that has been converted to a tourist stop with small cabins, a small wonderful restaurant and a herd of wild buffalo that roam the open mountainside.

The morning of our departure the buffalo herd had worked its way to an area near the restaurant while we were having our breakfast. As I observed the herd, I noted there was a black-and-white longhorn steer moving along with the 100 or so buffalo. Upon my inquiry, I found the story of Spot.

The black-and-white steer had been left behind in 1989 by the previous owners of Zion Mountain Ranch. The ranch then became the home of the buffalo herd that was introduced there by the new owners. It was at that time that Spot joined the herd. Being an impressionable young longhorn bull, Spot started his "transformation" into becoming a buffalo. He began to walk like a buffalo, talk like a buffalo and as far as he knows, never having looked into a mirror, looking like a buffalo.

Now, isn't our life just like the life of Spot in so many ways? We become like those we hang out with. If we hang out with turkeys we become a turkey. If we hang out with eagles we become eagles. The people we hang out with are our board of directors. They shape our lives, our future and even how we see ourselves. We can become who we expect ourselves to become. We should place our expectations of ourselves high. We need to raise our bar.

I share this belief system with each of you with the hope that we might each go forward with a commitment to be more fussy about who we share our time with. Let us each look to surround ourselves with folks who are better than us in the ways we have set our sights to become.

I would also hope we can share our talents by lifting others up whenever we are given the opportunity to do so. I would hope that we all would want to be the type of person that great people want to hang out with. As we travel through life's pathways, serving one another is what brings true joy.

Doug's Take:

Sharee and I joined a recent Harley Davidson excursion with Roy's foundation,

Learning Curves, where we traveled with a wonderful group of dentists to four national parks and two national monuments. While on the trip, one of our dentist riders had an unfortunate accident. He was cruising on one of the top 10 scenic rides in America from Torrey, Utah, down to Lake Powell, which takes you through Boulder Mountain, Escalante, Bryce Canyon and past Zion National Park. At one point, the highway drops off more than 1,000 feet on both sides of the highway. The scenery transforms from lush, green forest, to red rock sandstone. It is one of the most incredible rides that we do with Learning Curves.

This particular dentist, an experienced rider but mature in years, got so enthralled looking at the scenery that he rode his Harley Davidson right into the guardrail as he was looking off at the spectacular view. Roy needed to flag down help just to pull his Harley Davidson from being wedged under the guardrail. Thank goodness the rider had his leathers on and only had a few scrapes on his arm. Otherwise, it could have been a very ugly accident. (Luckily he was able to enjoy the remainder of the trip.) Just as Roy has pointed out, when we look at those things about us, we will go right to where our attention is focused.

THE ROAD TO HANA

As I mentioned, our family has a tradition of going to Maui on family retreats with a purpose in February of the odd years. If you have ever taken the road to the remote town of Hana on Maui, it is not only one of the most scenic rides in America, but also one of the most tedious. It is full of hairpin turns and curves in lush tropical foliage, laden with waterfalls along the coast—a four-hour ride from the main towns to get to Hana and then the same time to return. Most of the road you can only go about 15 miles per hour. That is why Hana sells thousands of T-shirts every year that have the phrase, "I Survived the Road to Hana".

On one particular trip we were all riding Harleys that we had rented. Even though we warned everyone to look ahead in the curves, it is another thing when you have a hairpin turn that has an upward incline. I have many times come close to dropping my motorcycle—it happens when you're too focused on the pavement where the front tire meets the road, rather than up the road. My son Aaron barely recovered from a near-fall on one very treacherous turn. Later as we rode down a side road to explore the jungle and ocean view, we got off the pavement for a few hundred feet, and Aaron again got too focused on the dirt in front of him and nearly crashed again. In frustration, he got off his Harley and kicked it. We all laughed as he quickly realized it was the rider, not the bike that was the problem. (In Aaron's defense, he is now an extremely skilled dirt biker and negotiates some of the most wicked terrain you can imagine—with grace and ease.) But again this illustrates, sometimes the wrong focus can do more than distract you—it can threaten long-term damage.

THE IMPACT OF OUR LOOKING AT OUR SURROUNDINGS

Have you ever heard the childhood phrase, "Monkey see, monkey do?" Well unfortunately we're all not too different from that monkey. We as humans subconsciously practice "reciprocity." We tend to adopt the behaviors, attitudes and choices of the people we surround ourselves with, the books we read, the media we consume. That's why, for example, parents worry when their children start spending time with a less than savory crowd—chances are their kids will mirror the actions of their friends. However, the converse is true, the better company we keep, the greater words we absorb, the better we tend to become. As we look ahead to our future, my guess is we'd all like to move toward a life of abundance. If so, it would do us well to assess the ideas and people we're bringing into our lives, because 10, 20, or 30 years from now, it will all have an impact on who we are.

Sharee and I have the wonderful opportunity of mentoring youth at a youth detention center. We get to spend at least one hour every Sunday and every Wednesday evening mentoring and mingling with these youth. At the detention center, there are usually about 30 young men that have committed some serious criminal offenses. They are in a lock-down facility. Some of them end up being there for extended periods of time—maybe two to four years. Oft times, these young men have been heavily involved in gangs, and many of them are sex offenders.

One of the reasons why the volunteers, a total of 32 of us, are so richly blessed and that our visits are so effective is because even though we know they have done something seriously wrong, we do not know the details of what they have done. Therefore, it's easy to mentor them with a non-judgmental attitude. Some of the greatest healers on the planet, historically, have not been physicians. The one common denominator is they were all non-judgmental.

Often, these young people simply grew up with a scarcity mindset that they learned in childhood. Many of them, as early as age five or six, were introduced to gangs, drugs and abuse. They have been told that there are haves and have-nots in the world, and that if the haves leave their garage door unlocked, they are the ones who did something wrong. This is an opportunity for them to go in and redistribute their property, tools, or belongings to the less fortunate—them. It takes sometimes six months to four years for these young boys to realize that what they have done is not acceptable, and that this mentality has often been a function of who they have been surrounded by.

My wife and I also get to mentor at boys' and girls' group homes, with 12- to 18-year-olds. Our goal is to help them avoid making more serious mistakes that would lead them to end up in a lock-down facility. And we have the opportunity to teach at Crisis Residential, a temporary residential facility where 12- to 18-year-old teenagers are often waiting to see a judge. They are in the middle of a crisis. Many of them have been attempting to take their life or their parents were arrested, and there is nowhere else for law enforcement officers to take them.

We also are lucky enough to serve at the Christmas Box House, a place for young children, ages zero to 12, who many times have been removed from abusive homes, as well as Early Intervention, a program where young people can stay at home, but they've been ordered by a judge to spend two to four hours every day learning responsibility and providing community service to prevent them from being assigned to a full-time residential facility.

It is clear how many of them of are simply a product of the people they have been surrounded by, including their families. And it is touching to see how much they love their brothers, sisters and parents, even though their life with them may have been rather miserable.

Even more, no matter their backgrounds, their past choices or their heartbreaking stories, it is inspiring to see how all of these young people brighten up when they learn more about having an abundance mentality.

While these government-run programs and facilities provide a remarkable service, more than just donating financially to causes like these, I have seen that the impact of volunteers giving of their time and talents has had far greater results on these young, impressionable people. Sometimes, it is simply the example they observe in couples like Sharee and I who interact in front of them. When I call Sharee "Sweetheart" or "Honey," it's simply a common term of endearment that is a part of our everyday communication with each other. But some of these young people come to us with tears in their eyes and say, "We love you volunteers coming, because we've never heard a husband and wife treat each other like you do! Is that what a marriage can really be like?"

ARE YOU A THRIVER OR SURVIVOR?

In my book, *Last Chance Millionaire,* (published in 2007, which I was blessed to have become a New York Times and Wall Street Journal Number One Best-Seller), I have a bell curve illustrated in the preface. It illustrates that in their lifetime, people—or even families through generations—go through a cycle that I call Strivers, Arrivers, Thrivers, Survivors, and Divers.

Unfortunately most people, the majority of Americans—the richest nation on earth—have a Striver mentality. This is really a scarcity mindset. They are always striving for happiness, thinking that life is unfair. They will have too much month left at the end of their money most of their life. They live in the moment. They borrow money to consume rather than to conserve. They are always striving for the magic bullet or the secret to their happiness, but they are not finding it through the accumulation of "things."

Arrivers begin to understand the secrets of wealth accumulation. But wealth—or what I call "Authentic Wealth" — is more than just the money. From a financial standpoint, those Arrivers understand compound interest, tax-favored savings, and safe, positive leverage. But these principles apply not just to money. They apply to a life of abundance.

The difference between Thrivers and Arrivers is that the Thrivers learn how to repeat the process over and over again. It's not just a one-off. They learn how to continue to grow both their financial wealth, as well as their foundational and intellectual assets. They never stop learning and achieving more.

No matter the category people find themselves in during their earning years, all too often things change for the worse when people begin to approach what we call "retirement." Now as a side note, I've never liked the word retirement, and here's why. The term came about during the Industrial Age, when factory workers who did the same thing over and over again ultimately were put out of use. They were retired, just like machinery, which only pushed them toward a Survivor mentality. That is why the average life expectancy for someone who was put out of use was only seven years for a male (six years for government retirees and only five years for military personnel).

If "retired" means "put out of use," I never want to be put out of use. The secret to longevity is making yourself necessary. Those who get into a Survivor mentality can worsen when they stop growing. They find that not only does their money run out, but also their health, their zest for living, their spirituality, their intellect, their brain, and they then become Divers. The Divers are the ones who pretty much become a self-fulfilling prophecy—they die when they make up their mind that they are going to check out.

I love helping people maintain a Thriver mentality, not only for themselves but for their children and grandchildren. This way they can avoid the mistake many wealthy families make when they transfer money to children and grandchildren. Too many families dump the financial treasure on ill-prepared heirs, and by the third generation, the money is usually all gone and they are back to rolling up their shirt sleeves again. Hence we have the saying "shirt sleeves to shirt sleeves in three generations."

So I'll ask, where do you see yourself? Are you already basking in the freedom that comes from being a Thriver? Are you on your way there, steadily making your way with the other Arrivers? Or are you lost in the crowd of Strivers, struggling and wondering why life is so tough? The great news is there's always hope. There's always the opportunity to learn more. You can always make changes. Turn your focus—your eyes on the road—to a brighter future. Put yourself on the path to abundance. Because you, too, deserve to thrive.

ABUNDANCE VS. SCARCITY—WHICH NEIGHBORHOOD DO YOU LIVE IN?

So, in the world there are givers and there are takers, the Thrivers versus the Strivers. Dan Sullivan, who I credited in Chapter 1, illustrates this by talking about those who live in the abundance neighborhood, versus those who live in a scarcity spiral.

He points out that the scarcity spiral begins with envy. When we focus on the achievements or wealth of others and we get jealous or upset because someone else seems more successful, we're in a mindset that somehow they took more than their fair share of happiness or accomplishments, and that leaves less for us.

That envy can lead to guilt, feeling ashamed that we haven't achieved the same level of success, which can lead to anger and resentment. We think thoughts like, "If you're wealthy and I'm not, that's not fair. They should redistribute the wealth so I can have more!" But this is a zero-sum mentality, believing that one person's gain comes at the expense of someone else's loss.

But think about it. If I take a breath right now out of the room ... does anyone else get bothered that I'm taking an extra breath away from the planet? No, because there's enough air to spare. There's abundance. Abundance breeds more abundance ... but some people don't understand that. They think that if you're successful, if you're happy, they cannot be happy.

If we ever head into that mindset, we've got to pull ourselves out and move over into the abundance neighborhood. The journey to this part of the map begins with gratitude. As we increasingly appreciate the value of everything and everyone we already have in our life, we naturally progress to the next stage, which is creativity and cooperation. We feel freer to add to the world rather than take away, to invent, to collaborate, to produce.

If you think about it, cooperation is actually what they should have named capitalism. Capitalism was named by its opponent, Karl Marx, who viewed it as capitalizing on people's needs and wants. But actually we're cooperating with each other, because if I can fish and you can grow corn and Suzie can sew the clothes, we cooperate, create an exchange, and that generates abundance.

From creativity and cooperation, we move on to exponential growth and greater ingenuity, which only opens doors for more opportunity ... all starting with that attitude of gratitude.

As you look at your own life, are you on the tracks toward ScarcityVille? Or are you bound for AbundanceLand? We are often a mix of the two, so it's important to identify the positive, assess the negative, and make changes so we can live completely in a place of abundance. Those who let scarcity take over end up in that spiral, which they pass on to their children and grandchildren. Wouldn't we rather pass on a legacy of creativity, gratitude, and abundance? Let's live a brighter life and extend that to our future generations, so everyone can thrive, versus just survive.

RANDOM OR PREDICTABLE? CHOOSE A PREDICTABLE PATH

As a financial strategist, over the past four decades I have worked with some of the nation's most successful, affluent achievers. These are the folks I've referred to in this chapter as Thrivers. Although they may have come from different backgrounds and circumstances—some started with a large inheritance, others were self-made—they all have something in common. And it's one of the biggest secrets to abundant living. But before I share that, I have a math exercise for you.

Pick a number, any number, between one and 10. Now take that number (the one you chose between one and 10), and double that number. Next add eight to that number. Now divide that number in half. What number do you have now? Next subtract the original number you started with from your latest number.

You should have a final number in your head now. Take that final number you arrived at and pick the corresponding letter of the alphabet that number represents. For example, if your last number was one, that would be the letter A. Two would be B; three would be C; four would be D; and so on. So what is your letter of the alphabet?

Now, take that letter of the alphabet and pick a country in Europe or the Baltics (using the American name for countries) that starts with that letter. It's going to be near the beginning of the alphabet, so you can choose from countries like England,

Germany, Ireland, France, Belgium, Czechoslovakia, Austria and Italy. Up in the Baltics, you've got Finland, Denmark, and Estonia.

Now, think of the country that starts with the letter of the alphabet you ended up with. Take that country, then think of the last letter of that country's name. Now pick a zoo animal—an animal that is not indigenous to the United States but one you'd probably find in a zoo in the United States—that starts with that letter (the last letter of your country you chose).

Do you have a zoo animal in your head? Now take the last letter of that zoo animal and pick a common fruit that starts with that letter, okay? So, you should have a country, a zoo animal and a common fruit.

Now, when I do this, I know what 80% of people are thinking: Denmark, kangaroo, orange. Is that what you thought? (Maybe you thought Denmark, koala, apple.) Either way, you're like 80% of people who perform this exercise.

Why is this? It's called predictability. Most of the time, 80% of people will get to these three items when they arrive at the number four. (If you did not get to four as the final answer on your number, then I hate to tell you, you may need to brush up on your math.)

What I love to do is teach people how to create predictability, so that no matter what you do, you have predictable systems. I like to point out that SYSTEM can be an acronym that stands for Save Your Self Time, Energy and Money.

I show people how to create predictability in their life to have the highest and best results with the least amount of effort. And when you do this consistently, with optimal information, you can enjoy abundant living.

Think about predictability in other terms. If you put this much wood in the fire, you'll get this many BTUs of heat back. If you follow this recipe for perfect cinnamon rolls at this particular altitude, 80-90% of the time you'll get a perfect batch of cinnamon rolls. If you teach your children the 12 concepts I outline in Chapter 12, 80 – 90% of the time they will be responsible-accountable-captains of their own souls-able to handle any curve ball life throws at them-self-reliant-never "unemployed" individuals.

Predictability may be fun in a math exercise. But how much more important is it when it comes to your financial well-being? Do you want to leave your most important life paths to chance? Or lazy math? Or random, follow-your-gut-and-the-rest-of-the-herd choices?

So, when you think of Denmark, kangaroo and orange, consider whether you're choosing the most predictable paths to abundant living. If not, there's no better time than the present to change your course by learning more, applying proven principles, and reaching your optimal destination.

It's all about where you look, where you keep your gaze. So while it's important to enjoy the journey and take in the view, avoid staring too long at the potholes, the guard rails and the seductive scenery. Keep your eyes on the road ahead, and make your way through a life of abundance.

RETHINK YOUR THINKING

U: ***How can YOU change your own life to ...***

- *"Hang out" with abundant-minded people?*
- *Feed your mind with positive affirmations?*
- *Be a Thriver—not a Striver?*
- *Counter envy with gratitude?*
- *Avoid the scarcity spiral and live in the proactive zone of predictable results?*

F: ***How can you help empower your close circle of FAMILY and FRIENDS to do the same?***

O: ***How can you influence OTHERS with whom you work and serve to do the same and become abundant-minded?***

IT'S NOT IF YOU ARE GOING TO FALL IT'S WHEN

3

Roy:

I have been riding motorcycles for 60 years now (now let's remember I started as a young kid!). In that time, I have had one serious fall that put me in the hospital. Without question, I have since been better prepared as a rider because of that fall. I learned I am not perfect; I am not invincible, that riding is an ongoing learning process, and that riding requires concentration on your surroundings at all times. The danger is always there and our job as riders, especially when you have a passenger behind you, is to do everything in your power to minimize the danger.

As you may know, my wife and I have founded an organization called Learning Curves (one of the many reasons even this book has special meaning for me). It's a charitable organization that brings dental professionals together for Harley Davidson tours and career development—and the funds go toward medical equipment and supplies we deliver on humanitarian missions around the world. To say this has been life-changing for my wife, our children and grandchildren—and the dentists and their staff involved—is an understatement. The people we've met, the courage they've shown, has been overwhelmingly inspiring. I could go on and on ... but in the interest of space, please visit **www.LearningCurvesBook.com** to learn more about our experiences.

Well, on one of our Learning Curves rides, I vividly recall one of our riders, due to his lack of focus, had a serious accident. When the Highway Patrol and emergency services arrived, the rider said to the police officer, "Well I guess my riding days are over." The officer replied, "No way, all of we riders fall sometime, and you got yours out of the way already. You have great riding years ahead."

Life is like that. We may think we are perfect, that we are invincible and will never fall, but that is not the case. I believe our Creator provided this "earthly journey" as a time to learn and grow, not only through our successes and accomplishments, but from our stumbles and our falls. Our job is to step back when we fall and ask, "Now, what can I learn from this situation? How can I be stronger in the future? How can I better serve others because of what I have learned from this experience?"

As we progress through life, have a spouse and children and then grandchildren, we are faced with an ever-greater responsibility to lessen our vulnerability to the distractions and dangers that surround us in all that we do. Our actions and our falls are going to affect future generations. Our children and grandchildren see us as their mentors. They see us as perfection and the person they want to be like when they grow up.

We are not perfect. There will always be bumps in the road, and we will always face times when we lose our balance. We can regain our balance and find our way back onto smooth pavement quickly—or we may fall hard. Either way, the thing to remember is that we can always get back up and go on.

Depending on how heavy the bike or the condition of the surface, it may be simple or very difficult to get the rubber back on the road. I have dropped my Harley a few times. This bike has a weight of around 800 pounds. It is nearly impossible for me to get it back upright alone. My wife and I are normally riding in groups. The blessing is that there are always others there to help put the bike back on its wheels.

Just the same, we need to realize that we can't do it alone. There are always parents, siblings, spouses, friends, ecclesiastical leaders and a Higher Power there to help. They want to help. There is joy in being in a helping relationship. Yes, we were always taught to be strong and independent, but it is not meant that we travel the bumpy roads of this life alone. Allow those who love you to have the joy of a helping relationship.

It seems like every time I fall and someone comes to help there is a comment like, "You know, I made that same mistake one time. Here's how I recovered, and here is what I learned from the challenge." Our falls and our recovery should make us wiser and stronger. We should then be better prepared to be a helper and a servant when our opportunity to do so comes along.

It is my hope that we might all be willing to receive help when we fall, and to learn from our mistakes. And may we also be ready and willing to lift others—even strangers—when they take their turn to fall.

Doug's Take:

My first fall with my Harley was within 30 minutes of it being uncrated from the shipping container. In 1999, I was on a business road trip through Texas. As you may be aware, driving through Texas from Houston to El Paso is a long haul on I-10. As we finally arrived in El Paso, Texas, we were attracted to the Barnett's Harley Davidson dealership, as it was touted by the signage as the Harley dealer with the world's largest selection. As we stopped, I was intrigued by the size and inventory of motorcycles—especially because this was an era when people had to pay a deposit and wait months or even a year or two for their Harley to be built. Demand was much greater than the supply. I quickly learned that all of the motorcycles in their showroom had been ordered many months earlier and they were simply "prepped" and on display, waiting for the people who had paid the deposit to pick up their bike and pay the balance.

There were about three Harleys that had been ordered by buyers who were now begging to back out, as they didn't have the funds to complete the purchase of the motorcycle. They took me in the back and uncrated one that I immediately took a liking to: a midnight metallic blue with silver diamond ice two-tone paint, Road King Classic (which has the leather saddle bags). I knew I had to have it—which was a blessing to the man who ordered it but could not pay for it, and a lucky day for me, as I was able to purchase it without the wait. I immediately had it shipped to my warehouse in Clearfield, Utah.

When my Harley arrived, my wife took me to the warehouse, which was about 30 minutes from our home in Salt Lake City. I uncrated the bike, mounted it and began my virgin ride on the back roads to Salt Lake City. I quickly realized the need to adjust the mirrors (which I was too nervous to do while riding), tie down a few things and ask my wife if my lights were working, so I pulled over on the shoulder. Well, the shoulder was full of loose gravel. I lost my footing and dropped my new bike. It took every bit of muscle and willpower for my wife and me to lift the bike upright again— especially on an uneven road full of gravel. (I have since learned how to do that much more efficiently.) I got my fall out of the way early, and now I'm extremely careful when, how and where I come to park my Harley, with full regard to how I'm going to negotiate getting back on the road again.

TOUCH ALL THE BASES IN LIFE

Looking at the falls, or setbacks, we make in life, we can also look at the game of baseball. Just like baseball, we have home plate, first, second, and third bases. Our most important—or home plate possessions—are our foundational assets—our family, health, values, talents, heritage, spirituality, future, etc. We also have another base comprised of our intellectual assets. Wisdom is a product of knowledge multiplied by experiences. And not just the good ones! I've learned more from my bad experiences in life. Other intellectual assets would include our formal education, reputation, systems, methods, traditions, alliances, skills, etc.

Next, would be our financial asset base—comprised of all of our material possessions—the things of life. The final base consists of our civic or social assets which we contribute back to society. Most governmental systems in the world have a method whereby be must give back to society, and that normally comes in the form of taxes. But there are ways that we can maintain choice and control by redirecting otherwise payable taxes when we take ownership and become self-sufficient rather than relying on government to take care of us. We can contribute our money, time, talents and other resources to many charitable causes. The point is: it's imperative that we touch all of the bases in life to stay balanced.

On September 23, 1908, in a game against the eventual World Series Champion Chicago Cubs, Fred Merkle, a 19-year-old rookie of the New York Giants, (yes, the name of the baseball team was the New York Giants at that time) was on first base and Moose McCormick was on third base.

There were two outs, and it was the bottom of the ninth inning with the score tied 1-1. The next batter, Al Bridwell, drilled an apparent single into center field. McCormick ran home from third, and the game appeared to be over, a 2–1 Giants victory. Giants fans poured out of the stands and mobbed the field. Merkle, advancing from first base, saw the fans swarming onto the playing field. He turned back to the dugout to join the celebration with his teammates without ever touching second. The Cubs' second baseman Johnny Evers noticed this, retrieved the ball, tagged second, and appealed to the umpire, who called Merkle out, nullifying McCormick's run.

The Giants and Cubs would finish tied atop the National League standings, and a one-game playoff was played to decide which team would win the Pennant. The Cubs would win this game, eliminating the Giants. Had the Giants won that September 23 game, the one-game playoff would have been unnecessary and the Giants may have won the same 1908 World Series that the Cubs proceeded to win.

The importance of touching all the bases was shown again at the start of the 1974 baseball season. Hank Aaron was a player with the Atlanta Braves team. He was seeking the record for hitting the most home runs. Aaron needed just one home run to equal the record held by Babe Ruth, the greatest hitter in baseball history. Aaron got that home run the very first time he had a chance to hit the ball. He sent the ball over the wall. That gave him seven hundred and fourteen home runs—the same as Babe Ruth.

After that day, baseball fans held their breath every time it was Hank Aaron's turn to hit. When would he hit home run number seven hundred and fifteen? The wait wasn't long. In the second week of the season, Aaron again hit the ball over the wall. He had beaten Babe Ruth's record. But first, he had to run around the four bases. The other players on his team watched carefully to make sure he touched each one. If he did not, the home run would not have counted. There would have been no new record. To Hank Aaron's credit he made it home.

To make sure your home runs will count in life, remember to touch all of the bases—and don't stop with just the foundational, intellectual and financial bases. You'll only score a triple if you don't pay it forward by contributing of your means to others and come back to "home" to make it all count. And if you blow the game a few times by missing a base? Get your uniform back on and play another day. You just might beat your own record!

ARE YOU ON OR OFF?

Thomas Edison is one of the most famous, incredible inventors in history. He was an abundant-minded scientist. A young reporter came to him after he had attempted over 10,000 times to invent the electric light bulb (for which he is most famous), and asked, "How does that feel, Mr. Edison, having failed 10,000 times?" Edison said, "You're young; you don't understand. I have not failed 10,000 times. I have successfully found 10,000 ways that don't work." He went on to make over 6,000 more attempts before he invented the electric light bulb, and look at how many lives have been blessed on this planet.

Edison also invented several other things. In my opinion, I think his greatest contribution was the telegraph. You see, after inventing the telegraph, people on the east coast on Wall Street could learn within six or seven seconds when to buy, and when to sell. It changed communication on this planet. Edison approached the problem of communicating the complicated 26 letters of the English alphabet through Morse code with just two different signals: a dot and a dash. He had to solve how many dots and dashes, and in what sequence, would compose letters, words and sentences.

When you think about it, this was really the precursor to digital technology, or what we know as binary language. In other words, is the signal a one, or a zero? It's also essentially what makes television work. Each of those tiny little LED lights are either on or off, or the degree in which they are on brings out to the human eye the color that we perceive. When digital technology first came out in the 70s, I remember my first calculator. Every letter or number could be illustrated with a series of seven LED lights; these are known as bits of information. Depending upon which LED bars were lit up or which were dark, it could be construed as a digital character, or a byte of information. The eighth bit that comprises a byte is the entire symbol; hence, eight bits make one byte of information.

If you've ever seen the photograph of mother Earth from outer space, the Korean peninsula is very visible from outer space. South Korea, no bigger than the state of Utah, appears lit up like Las Vegas. From space, it is "ON." They have entrepreneurism. They allow ownership. In 60 years they have recovered from the Korean War with freedom. They produced the number one selling automobile in the world in the year 2013, Hyundai, which surpassed Toyota. In contrast, North Korea is dark and austere. There's only one light perceivable from space, and that is from the presidential compound. The citizens are not allowed to own private property. The government makes all their decisions for them and owns everything. I think this illustrates why they are starving, and why they threaten the world with nuclear warfare unless we constantly help them. The difference between North Korea and South Korea boils down to Survivors and Thrivers in the bell curve that I've illustrated.

If you're understanding my point, I think we're all really that simple. In most of the classics, and especially in scripture, this is what God (the Universe, or whatever your belief of a Higher Power) is really asking: Are you on, or off? Are you with me, or against me? Are you abundant-minded, or are you scarcity-minded? Do you see the glass half-full, or half-empty? Are you a pessimist, or an optimist? Do you brighten the room when you enter it, or when you leave it? If you find yourself on the dimmer side of the spectrum, then count it as your "fall" in life, put the rubber back on the road and start heading toward a brighter future.

FLIP THOSE FLAWS

Do you sometime get hung up on your flaws, or muddled down by life's challenges? If you do, you're in good company. Most people get at least temporarily waylaid by difficulties, but like we've been talking about, it's what we do after the initial negative impact that matters most. Whether it's in business, with our families, or in our personal endeavors, we don't have to be held back by our mistakes or setbacks. We can flip them ... with something I call the "negative experience transformer."

I developed a seven-step process for turning life's negatives into positives a few years ago. First, we've got to look at our mindset. How are we looking at the issue? A pessimist is a person who sees challenges in every opportunity, where on the other hand the optimist is a person who sees the opportunities in every challenge. There's also the saying, "When the going gets tough, the tough get going." And I love the quote from Gene Kranz, the legendary NASA flight controller who led the effort to save the Apollo 13 mission, when he said, "Failure is not an option."

Next, we take that mindset check to the next level by doing a gratitude assessment. In other words, you want to identify those things that you are grateful for. This helps us get out of that victim mentality. If you think about it, the word appreciate means to increase in value. It also means to fully understand the circumstances. As you appreciate what you have—both the good and the bad—your whole life can appreciate in every sense of the word.

The next step in this process is to gain the proper perspective. It's important to always keep the big picture in mind, reminding ourselves this is a small moment in time. We can ask ourselves, "What can I learn from this?" An anonymous writer once penned, "It's often the view from where you sit that makes you fear defeat. Life is full of many aisles so why don't you change your seat?"

The next step is to deal with our setbacks by incorporating faith, hope and charity, which I'll talk about in Chapter 11. Essentially it means to replace fear with faith, to look for hope in our ability to resolve the situation, and to approach ourselves—and others—with love that extends beyond frustration or offense over the current situation.

Next, we've got to get out of ourselves and realize in this world of constant global change, people are always feeling confused and isolated and powerless. We need to ask ourselves, "How can I help other people get the clarity, confidence and capability they need to clear up that confusion, isolationism and powerlessness?" We do that with leadership, relationships and creativity. This particular insight came from my friend, Dan Sullivan. The great part about this? If you help other people get their canoe across the pond; your canoe gets across the pond.

At this point you'll be ready for the final steps, which are to: 1) consciously train your mind and body to unconsciously act in harmony with your family values and vision by doing an R Factor question, and 2) perform a DOS analysis (which will help you eliminate the dangers, seize the greatest opportunities and harness the greatest strengths of the situation). These steps are so critical—and so intensive—that I will cover them in more detail in future chapters.

Essentially, by following these steps, we can take any negative experience or flaw, flip it into a positive and then turn it into intellectual capital that we can then pass on to employees, family and associates. And when we do this regularly? We get even farther ahead than if the setback had never happened, and that's powerful, abundant living!

BLESSED ARE THE FLEXIBLE—DON'T GET BENT OUT OF SHAPE!

You've seen it, haven't you? You're in a management meeting, addressing a challenge the company is facing, and the executive overseeing that aspect of the business won't hear it.

Despite the evidence that the current approach isn't working, regardless of the viable options others are recommending, he just can't imagine handling the issue any other way. So he digs in his heels and insists on doing things the way they've always been done. Sure enough, down the road the damage is so undeniable that he eventually caves and allows for other solutions – but it may be too little too late.

Blessed are the flexible, for they shall not be bent out of shape. This is sort of my own personal beatitude, and time and again I've seen it apply to so many aspects of business and life. Let me illustrate with this example. If you were to take off from Salt Lake City International Airport where I live in Utah, headed for an around-the-world journey right back to Salt Lake, what would happen if you started one degree off course? If you never corrected that one degree, you would be 500 miles from your take-off point when you returned. That's how much of a difference just one degree can make.

I apply this principle to a lifetime of teaching people how to save and invest. I have long insisted on flexibility in one's financial planning, so if at any time life throws a curve ball, you can redirect your course and get back on track. Maintaining the utmost liquidity is critical so you can have access to your cash, make changes, put more money aside, or take money out without a penalty.

On a Harley ride, when we have an unexpected breakdown, a flat tire, or other mishap, we have learned you've got to stay calm and be extremely flexible, because those problems *will* occur. It also helps in going into hairpin turns or bumpy roads—if you tense up, you're more likely to fall. Keep that fluid attitude and those loose limbs going, and you'll enjoy the ride a lot more.

RETHINK YOUR THINKING

U: *How can YOU ...*

- *Be more accepting of life's challenges?*
- *Be assured that falling and failing in life are inevitable and are necessary for learning?*
- *Know that if we touch all the bases, stay on board, flip the flaws and remain flexible, we can overcome and be up and doing again?*

F: How can you help empower your close circle of FAMILY and FRIENDS to do the same—and realize that falling occasionally in life is part of life's learning process (and it is nothing to be ashamed of)?

O: How can you support and encourage OTHERS with whom you work and serve to do the same?

IT'S NOT HOW HARD YOU FALL IT'S HOW YOU RECOVER

4

Roy:

When you're riding an 800-pound plus bike, trust me, nobody wants to fall. But as we've pointed out, you're not going to get down many roads without at least one good spill. In fact, you can count on several falls, but the key is how well you recover.

I remember the one serious fall I had on my bike. My wife and I were on a high mountain road near where we live. I entered a tight curve, taking it too wide onto the shoulder. I had to lay the bike down to avoid going off the cliff that was just past the shoulder. My wife and I both had on our helmets and leather jackets, but I had only my jeans to cover my legs. My knee hit the pavement, and the pavement first removed my jeans, then it removed all of the tissue covering my knee. Well, I had always been taught that you do what you gotta' do in life, with no debate.

After recovering my composure, we unbent a few parts of the bike to make it workable. I wrapped my T-shirt around my knee to stop the bleeding. We got the bike back onto the road and got it into second gear. It was my left knee that had been injured and had to be kept out of use, so I couldn't shift gears. With my wife behind me on the bike, we started our one-and-a-half hour journey in second gear back to the hospital in our town.

After two hours of surgery to graft and mend the skin and tissue over the knee, they placed a drain in my knee, and I had to keep it immobile for six weeks while the site healed. This would have been hard, but even harder was that my wife and I were scheduled the next week to travel to Bora Bora to give a lecture during a seminar there.

We had to traverse several airports with me in a wheelchair, and I was assigned the bulkhead seat on each plane so I could place my leg out straight (in the hold where babies usually lie). We finally made it to Bora Bora, where we had to drain and rewrap my knee every night, but I was committed to giving all my lectures. Likewise, when we returned I kept up with my patient schedule despite having to keep my knee immobilized. After all, it wasn't their fault I had the accident. The very next day after the restraining wraps were removed, I made it a point to get back on my Harley—but this time as a wiser, more careful rider.

I remember my first wife, Frances, riding 3,500 miles for 10 days with her arm in a sling (nursing a rotator cuff tear). Despite the pain and inconvenience, she was dedicated to completing our hosting of a Learning Curves ride and waited until our return to have surgery. (And my second wife, Glenda, went body surfing and snorkeling in Hawaii on our honeymoon, without ever sharing with me her deep fear of the ocean. Brave women!)

But these are just mostly just physical falls. Without question, I think our emotional falls can prove to be our greatest challenges for recovery. When I suddenly lost Frances, my wife of 48 years, to a long-standing illness, I was personally lost. I had no hope of recovery. My heart and spirit were broken. It was not a fall where I could just wrap my T-shirt around my knee and ride away.

Many long, thoughtful days and nights were spent looking for a path to recovery. Many prayers were offered asking for strength and guidance. One of my most powerful lessons from this experience is that there is always help when we seek it—help through family, through friends, and through prayer. My strength and hope and joy were restored when my wife, Glenda, came into my life. She has been my key to recovery from the unimaginable fall. We cannot be all that we are meant to be by going the path alone. A true partnership should give strength to both people beyond their individual capacity, and I'm grateful to have been blessed enough to have had two incredible partners.

Now there is yet another fall that we may not have considered. While riding to Sturgis a few years ago, an inexplicable accident occurred. The wife of one of our good friends in the group veered off the road, crashing through a grassy burrow. All the while her husband, who was riding behind her on his bike, watched in horror and grief—not being able to do anything, not knowing what had happened. The good news is that her injuries were minor, and the major damage was to the bike.

This is not unlike the burden on a parent or grandparent, watching the fall of a child or grandchild and knowing there is nothing they can do. This fall could be from a result of making a personal choice or from consequences of someone else's decisions. We all go through life knowing that we can't fix other people, no matter how much we love them or how much we would like to change them. It's times like these our continued love and our prayers for help from our Creator are our only hope.

When we have learned to commit ourselves to move ahead in life, staying focused on our commitment to friends, family and our Creator—no matter what obstacles we encounter—we are on the road to ultimate success and recovery from any falls. I hope I can continue to see my falls as opportunities to learn and grow, which will only help me be a better husband, father and grandfather.

Doug's Take:

As I mentioned in an earlier chapter, the first year I owned a motorcycle, my Honda 125 back in 1974, is when I had my first serious fall. Later that same year, my brother Sherm borrowed a Suzuki 400 from a friend, and we went to ride in the clay pits above Provo, Utah. There were several dirt bikers there that day, all riding up and around the hills. One particular hill was the tallest, and to show you were really courageous, you had to ride your bike up that hill and jump through the air. I didn't have experience at doing this, but I'm always game to try. After riding up the hill successfully and easing off the gas as I "topped out," everyone was booing because I wasn't getting any air. So I attempted the climb again and again, with more and more "guts," until I was getting spectator approval for the amount of air I was getting.

The surface area on top of the hill was very small. So once you recovered from your landing, you had to be immediately prepared to go down the other steep side of the hill. I was novice at this, but I was also feeling pretty confident in my newly discovered skills. Well, Sherm asked if I wanted to try riding the Suzuki 400 (substantially more powerful). I hesitated but said, "Sure!" So off I went up the hill with such incredible power that I quickly realized I was in over my head. I could hear the crowd holler approval as I flew high over the jump at the top, but I never came back around to greet their applause.

I flew so high that I didn't come back to earth until I was heading down the hill on the opposite side. I panicked in the air and pulled back. I hit the ground on my tailbone and my back. To make matters worse, as I tried to brace the fall with my gloved hands against the clay gravel, the motorcycle came down on top of me. As I slid down the hill, the leather gloves ripped through, the flesh peeled off the palms of my hands and the gravel embedded itself. I hurt everywhere—for days!

I hobbled into the emergency room. The doctor did his best to clean the wound and get every bit of gravel that he could detect, scrubbing and scraping at my swollen hands. A week or so later, I was in for a checkup. The doctor noticed a small black piece of gravel that he had missed at the base of my left palm. He asked if I wanted him to dig it out. Remembering the joy of my previous visit, I asked, "If it is left there, will it bother me?"

He assured me that the gravel would likely not be any concern and that it would probably only be detectible to me—like a miniature "tattoo." Well, I'm not a fan of tattoos. I've always believed them to be a permanent reminder of a temporary feeling. But on this occasion I left the tiny piece of gravel in my hand. It is still barely detectible today, 40 years later. Every time I look at it, it reminds me not to pull back when I encounter challenges, but rather to push forward. You see, had I pushed forward, I could have landed that fall and recovered far more easily (and think of the cheers *that* would have gotten!).

LESSONS FROM DISNEY

Two of my family's favorite places to go are Disneyland and Disney World. Part of our love affair is because of our admiration for Walt Disney, who was an incredible man. He actually went broke about six or seven times and suffered a nervous breakdown before he finally made it. He admits that his salvation was that little mouse originally named Steamboat Willie, who later became Mickey Mouse. Mickey Mouse has been the number one entertainer in America for over 70 years. (Unlike the stock market, Mickey never has a down year.)

We talk about all the incredible things that Walt Disney did. Did you know that his brother vetoed the idea for Mickey—in fact, many of the ideas that Walt had? But Walt knew when he had criticism from naysayers, he was on to something. Who do we remember and revere? Walt's brother? Do you remember his name? Very few people know his brother was named Roy. (He wasn't like my brother Roy who is co-authoring this book; he's a possibility-thinker.) The world does remember Walt, however, because he learned how to pick himself up after his failures and succeed.

When our family goes to Disneyland, one of our favorite rides is Pirates of the Caribbean. Even though this ride was created years ago, it still remains one of our must-rides. When Walt Disney finished constructing the ride, he had all of his employees experience it. At the end, he assembled all of them on the deck of the Blue Bayou Cafe to get their feedback. You see, one of the secrets to Walt Disney's success is that he always made his cooperation greater than his status. In other words, he made every performance greater than the recognition or the applause that he would get (these are also lifetime principles included in Dan Sullivan's book, *The Laws of Lifetime Growth*).

Two of the young black girls that were in the kitchen did not think that he meant for them to come also. He asked where they were and the staff had to go retrieve them, because he wanted everybody's contribution. When it was their turn to speak, they were asked what was missing on the ride. One of them said shyly, "Well Mr.

Disney, were I come from, there are fireflies. I didn't see any fireflies." Disney said, "Brilliant!" and he called engineering and said, "We need to figure out how to make some fireflies." How many of you enjoy those fireflies on that ride? Then the next little black girl got courage and said, "Well Mr. Disney, where I come from there are swamps. This does not smell like a swamp." Again, that was brilliant, and he got engineering to create the ambience and odors of a swamp. Disney understood that it was much better to cooperate than to simply think that he knew everything. He made is cooperation greater than his status—another great lesson from this American icon.

LESSONS FROM STEVE JOBS

One of the most fascinating people that I study is Steve Jobs. As you may be aware, he did not achieve his ultimate success until the second time he came back to Apple. Steve had the ability to create value and deliver things that people wanted. (This is something that I teach in my three-day Clarity Experiences, where people come to discover principles they may not have been aware of before. They often end up wanting something they did not know they wanted until they had experienced it.)

Steve was a master at this. But it wasn't until the last seven years of his life that he really got it. (In fact, what is amazing is that within 48 hours of his passing, much of the world learned about his death reading the news on one of the devices he helped develop or inspired others to develop.)

Steve Jobs learned that negative experiences and criticism were actually the best research and development he could ask for. You see, Steve Jobs did not invent the cell phone. He just made a better one. He created one of the most popular cell phones and platforms, which people in turn used to create more value by combining their unique apps with his platform. As of the printing of this book, the Apple store has more than 1.2 million apps. During the iPhone-6 launch weekend, Apple sold 25-times more CPU transistors (in one weekend) than were in all the PCs on earth in 1995. In 1992, you could expect to pay $222 for a computer with 1 million transistors. Today, 1 million transistors cost a measly 6 cents. Today the average chip in your cell phone can perform about a billion calculations per second. Four billion people are buying new smartphones every two years, massively outpacing the PC industry (where we buy 1.6 billion PCs every five years). In the next five years, 80% of the adults on earth will have a smart phone. Wow!

Likewise Steve Jobs did not invent the MP3 player. But when he saw the technology, he thought, wow, thousands of songs in everybody's pocket. At the time, the music industry viewed him as a threat. They resisted his idea that people could download a song on iTunes for 99 cents. He said no, you will sell more music. This will explode the music industry. They thought it would destroy the music industry—people needed to buy 12 songs on an album to support the industry, right? Well they were scarcity-minded. Now the music industry is forever grateful for the technology and the ability for people to purchase songs. I have purchased the same tune numerous times for different devices, even though I could go to my original file. Why? Because he created convenience and value.

When he first came out with the iPod, critics said that's too big. For joggers, they didn't want a heavy device strapped to their arm. Steve Jobs basically said thank you for that criticism, and he came out with the iPod Nano. Some criticized that it was still too long. So he came out with the Shuffle.

When he came out with the idea of the iPad, many critics said, "Who wants a tablet? We have laptops. We have PDAs. We have desktops." Well he went ahead with his idea and sold millions of iPads. (The Andrew family is among those purchasers. One day on a Sunday afternoon after we had christened one of our grandchildren at church, our entire family was gathered. I counted 11 iPads in our living room, primarily being dominated by the grandkids. That technology has allowed people to apply all kinds of apps for learning, games and other useful tools that have changed the world for the better.)

Critics of his early iPad said that it was too big. Jobs said thank you for that input, and he came out with the iPad Mini, one that could fit in your purse. I am grateful because I have over 154 DVD educational videos that are in my 100-hour library. I combined my library on an iPad Mini that holds 64 gigs, and now people can become educated on ways to live the abundant life.

And with everything he introduced, Steve Jobs had taken negative feedback and turned it into his next incredible breakthrough. By combining resources with ingenuity, he, and all who have contributed to the technology and applications since, have created abundance.

HOMAN J. WALSH & THE KITE THAT HELPED BUILD A BRIDGE

When Homan J. Walsh died in Lincoln, Nebraska, on March 8, 1899, local newspapers noted that he had been a 30-year resident of the city, a real estate businessman, officer of the Lincoln Gas Company, and a past city council member. Of greater interest to Nebraskans, both then and now, was Walsh's unique boyhood contribution to the building of the first suspension bridge over the Niagara River. The Nebraska State Journal, as well as other newspapers around the country, used the occasion of his death to recall the unusual story for readers.

In 1848 Walsh, then a boy in New York state, played a key role in the construction of the first suspension bridge across the Niagara River between the United States and Canada. In the fall of 1847, civil engineer Charles Ellet, Jr. of Philadelphia was commissioned to construct such a bridge at the narrowest point of the Niagara gorge, immediately above the Whirlpool Rapids. Ellet was about to begin when he faced his first obstacle. The building of a suspension bridge is begun with the stretching of a line or wire across the stream. However, the turbulent rapids, the 800-foot-wide gap, and the 225-foot-high cliffs of the Whirlpool Gorge made a direct crossing impossible.

It occurred to someone that a kite might be a way to bridge the chasm. Accordingly, a cash prize was offered to the first boy that could fly his kite, with a line attached, to the opposite bank. There was a tremendous turnout of American and Canadian boys for a contest held in January 1848. The first to succeed in spanning the gorge with his kite, named the Union, was a young American, Homan J. Walsh.

In order to take advantage of more favorable winds, Walsh crossed to the Canadian side of the gorge by ferry just below Niagara Falls, and walked the two miles along the top of the cliff to the bridge site. At midnight, when a lull in the wind occurred, he flew his kite high above the gorge, and it reached the American side.

Then there was a sudden pull of the line, and it went limp. It had broken. To make matters worse, Walsh found himself marooned in Canada for eight days because river ice prevented the ferry from operating.

Finally Walsh was able to cross to the American side of the river and retrieve his kite. He then returned to the Canadian side, where he again flew the kite to the opposite bank. The kite string was fastened to a tree on the American shoreline, and a cord attached to it was pulled across. This time it didn't break. Next came a heavier cord, then a rope, and finally a wire cable, which was the beginning of the new bridge, completed on July 26, 1848.

Sometimes, the building of a strong bridge between generations or people on opposite sides starts with a small string and persistence as the ties become stronger and stronger.

FROM BIG ROCK TO MASTERPIECE

We've all heard the questions. Are you an optimist or a pessimist? A glass is half-full or half-empty kinda' person? But maybe there's more to it all than simply positive or negative perspectives—maybe it's what we see when others don't. Perhaps it's those who see possibilities in impossibilities who succeed. The folks who find the opportunity in the challenge, rather than the challenge in the opportunity. These are the people who can help create change for themselves—and for the world around them.

One of my favorite stories to illustrate this is that of the Malibu Rock. Back in 1977, Brett Livingston Strong immigrated to America from Australia to try to eke out a living as an artist. While living in a humble Los Angeles apartment he watched a story unfold on the news for several weeks. The story was of a homeowner who had built a beautiful home on Malibu Beach, but was worried about a big rock protruding on the cliffs. He and his neighbors were banding together to file a lawsuit to ask the state of California to move the rock, for fear that it could cause serious damage in an earthquake. Finally, they succeeded and coerced the state of California to move this rock.

Strong saw the opportunity here. He went down to witness this thing. Caltrans, who worked all morning to remove this rock, finally broke it loose early in the afternoon. The rock got away from them, and it landed smack dab in the middle of U.S. Pacific Coastal Highway 1. The crews had no idea what to do with a 116-ton rock blocking traffic in both directions.

Strong walked up and offered to buy the rock for $100. He met with some disbelief, especially when he explained all he had on him was $1, and he would pay for the rest later. The engineer told him he could have the rock, as long as he found a way to move it.

Strong went down to a shopping center and convinced the mall management to pay for a crane and helicopter to move this rock. In return he would lease it to them for six months in the center court of their mall while he went to work on it with a hammer and a chisel. They saw the publicity opportunity in it and agreed.

Strong went to work on the rock, and six months later it was ready to unveil. Everyone was curious when he brought a man from Orange County in a wheelchair to attend the event. As he pulled the drape from the rock, there was the image of John Wayne, the western cowboy movie star.

The man in the wheelchair leaned back and said, "I like it." It was John Wayne, just three weeks before he died of cancer.

Strong sold that statue carved into the Malibu rock for $1.1 million, and his career went through the roof.

A good friend of mine, Richard Rossi, says that when there's anxiety in the world, it spells opportunity. Develop the skill to see the possibilities in challenges. Become one of the few who carves paths—or masterpieces—through obstacles. Create an incredible career—and help others do the same—by leading the way.

DETOURS TO BETTER PATHS

I'm often asked about my journey to bestselling author, national speaker and financial strategist. This is where I tell a story—one that just may provide a helpful perspective as you look at your past, and your future. And from my own experience I can say that what looks at first like an unwanted detour, can actually lead to a better path.

In 1978, a young married couple built their third home in central Utah. It was their "dream home." It had 6,400 square feet, cathedral-beam—wood-decked ceilings, and a master bedroom deck where they could watch the deer and elk bed down in the scrub oak below them. They thought they had the world by the tail! Two years later in 1980 a bad recession hit America. That year in Houston, Texas during the energy crisis, 16,000 homeowners lost their homes in foreclosure. 16,000 people didn't all of a sudden become "bad people"—they just couldn't make their mortgage payments.

Well, the recession rippled across America, Utah included. This couple experienced three major setbacks that they never imagined would happen at once, and they found themselves without an income. So they got behind on their mortgage payments. Fortunately, they owned a rental duplex and they sold it and took the equity and brought the delinquent mortgage current. Then they got behind again. They owned a timeshare at a ski resort that they sold for triple what they had paid for it and were able to bring the delinquent mortgage current a second time. But realizing they had no other liquid assets, and not seeing any light at the end of the tunnel in the foreseeable future, they decided to sell their house.

They listed their home for sale for $295,000, because it had appraised four years earlier for $305,000. No takers. When supply is greater than demand, real estate values plummet. They quickly lowered the price several times to $285,000, $275,000, $265,000; then down to $225,000 and even $195,000; but to no avail. They will never forget the day they went to the county courthouse in Provo, Utah, and on the steps at the Sheriff's auction, they watched their beautiful home get auctioned off in foreclosure proceedings. My wife and I were that couple.

The experience of losing a house in foreclosure was a defining moment for me as a financial strategist and retirement planning specialist. What have been some of the results of this defining moment?

I no longer take all financial advice for fact, and you shouldn't either.

I look through the LENS of my own experience—because a truth is just a belief until you experience it.

I don't follow the herd with regard to my money, and I don't pay much attention to the mainstream media because they are part of the herd.

You see, I've discovered that the three key elements of any and all prudent investments are 1) liquidity (the ability to access your money when you need it), 2) safety of principal, and 3) rate of return. And real estate equity failed all three.

Now I keep all of my financial assets positioned with liquid access, safe and earning predictable, tax-favored rates of return, so that no matter what happens in the stock market or real estate market, I don't lose. This focus that I developed has helped me and thousands of others I've shared this wisdom with to avoid losing during tough times.

The world loves usefulness. You will be compensated for sharing your wisdom. People from all over the planet have read that story in my books or online and have sent me thank you notes for sharing because it helped them from making the same mistake.

THAT WHICH DOESN'T KILL YOU ...

Three months after we were first married, Sharee conceived our first child. During the first trimester of that pregnancy, Sharee was deathly sick and was in so much pain that it required hospitalization. She could not hold anything down. The doctors finally assumed she had a gallstone that was not passing. Even though there was danger that she would miscarry, they finally decided they needed to go in and remove the gallstone and/or the gallbladder. When they opened her up, to their shock and surprise, they found a football-sized cholodocal cyst that was intermeshed between her liver and pancreas. Three and a half hours later, they had drained it down to the size of a grapefruit. In frustration, they closed her back up again, not knowing what else they could do.

Sharee ended up having several more serious episodes of pancreatitis and cholangitis during the remaining six months of our first child's development. She was in intensive care several times, nearly passed away, and had had extensive pain meds. The doctor was Roy Hammond's father, Doctor Roy B. Hammond, who not only had delivered Sharee when she was born, but also five of our six children. He had delivered thousands of other babies. When our oldest daughter, Mailee, was born, he literally wept and said that he never dreamed our baby would be normal because of the trauma that Sharee had been through during that pregnancy.

Long story short, Sharee had numerous other surgeries, some for issues so dire the doctors did not believe that Sharee would make it. She ended up in intensive care on many occasions for weeks.

We have at times been very frustrated, wondering why we were going through this tremendous trial. But in retrospect, even though Sharee has suffered through tremendous physical trials, we know that had they tried to solve it earlier, that it would have probably taken her life. Today, she still has occasional setbacks, but at age 60-plus, Sharee is stronger than ever and can outdo any of her daughters at the fitness center. She has an enormous amount of compassion and patience that she has developed through her challenges. Even though there aren't always answers—or even relief—some of our greatest successes come with the greatest challenges, in God's own way, and in His own time-frame.

There's a saying, "That which doesn't kill you makes you stronger." Fortunately for all of us, Sharee's setbacks have only helped make her stronger, just as recovering from any fall on a motorcycle—or life—can do if we turn it around and make it a positive.

RETHINK YOUR THINKING

U: *How can YOU develop the ability to . . .*

- *Bounce back after every fall or setback in life and recover stronger than before?*
- *Take negative criticism as critical research and development?*
- *Stick to the task regardless of hang-ups?*
- *See the opportunity in the threat and eventually make your gratitude greater than the ultimate success?*

F: How can you empower your close circle of FAMILY and FRIENDS to do the same—supporting them in recovering from their own falls and setbacks in life by not just bailing them out of the problem, but by empowering them to solve their own problems? And by giving them a hand up instead of a handout?

O: *How can you encourage OTHERS with whom you work and serve to do the same?*

5 HEAVY LOAD ... TOUGHER RIDE

Roy:

Over the years, I've noticed I feel a completely different challenge in safely maneuvering the bike, depending on the type of trip and load I'm carrying.

If I'm heading out on my one-up seat for a day-ride with one of my sons, it's worlds apart from when the bike is loaded, with my sweet wife and our luggage on the back. I instinctively feel all the weight and her safety are in my hands. My approach is more attuned, and my concerns much more heightened. As long as the road is smooth or straight, I can relax a little. But when there are bumps in the road or we encounter curves, every one of those challenges is magnified.

Life is like that. I remember cruising through my elementary school years free as a bird. Then came junior high school and high school, and the only care in the world I had was if I was popular, if my hair was combed just right, or if all of the wrinkles were ironed out of my shirt. Oh, and of course, I had to be wearing the correct aftershave.

For me, grades in school came easy. Too much social life and no time to study? Not a problem. I could sail through it without much work, and if I didn't do that well, no big deal. But then my first quarter of college caught me off guard. The realities of life were now staring me in the face. I was not prepared for the bumps and the curves, and I had a pretty good crash. I recovered by going into the military and heading back to school afterward, but I learned a valuable lesson.

When I was married a few years later, I began to really feel the weight. I had the responsibility of a very special passenger. But then the load got even heavier when we added children to the mix, with those trusting new young spirits looking to me to be perfect, to be their mentor, to be the caretaker of their mother. And then in time, grandchildren came. Even though my children by now had discovered that I wasn't perfect in any sense of the word, they knew I would always give my best. (Now the great-grandchildren are on the way, and I only hope I am up to the task.)

GIVE UP OR KEEP GOING?

As the load of life's realities are added around every turn in life, it would be easy to give up, lose focus, and then lose the balance in our lives that keeps the rubber side down. Since the day I committed to be a husband and a future father, grandfather and great grandfather, I have committed myself to balancing the load no matter how heavy it becomes. But it hasn't always been easy, to say the least. As I explained earlier, when I lost my wife of 48 years and was left alone, I did lose my balance for a period of time. That was the most difficult right-hand, uphill, hairpin curve I could have ever imagined. The blessing is that one year later my new wife was there on the passenger seat encouraging, supporting and loving me back upright and into balance.

We all need that passenger on the back. Whether it's a spouse, a child, friends or community members, sharing the journey is where the joy is. The added responsibility that comes with a passenger may make the journey more challenging, but my life experiences have convinced me, without a doubt, that it will always make the journey much better when we take trusted folks along for the ride.

Doug's Take:

Roy's birthday usually falls on Sturgis week, so he often likes to enjoy the journey to the Black Hills of South Dakota. Sharee and I had never been to Sturgis or Mount Rushmore, but Roy and Glenda asked if we would like to accompany them in 2011—just two bikes—to experience the incredible sights. We didn't lodge in Sturgis; we stayed at a very nice lodge in Keystone at the base of Mount Rushmore, and we visited the town of Sturgis and Rapid City's Harley Dealership to see the unbelievable amount of motorcycles, displays and vendors that are on sight. I've never witnessed anything like it before. Other bike rallies are spectacular, but Sturgis is stupendous.

We took three days to get to South Dakota, stayed there four nights and took three more days to get back home. (I have learned that you should pack as lightly as possible unless you have a chaser vehicle.) We didn't have a chaser, so every bit of clothing and gear for 10 days had to fit on our bikes. Now, Sharee and I both together weigh less than 285 pounds, but I'm convinced we had about that much weight again in leathers and luggage on that first trip to Sturgis. I had two saddlebags loaded, two duffle backs strapped to the tops of the two saddlebags, two backpack T-bags behind us, and two roll bags strapped on top of the backpacks. After a stop, it was truly a balancing act just to get the bike going until we gained enough speed to keep from wobbling. Indeed, when the load is heavy the balance is more difficult. (We even had to put more air in our shocks because we were bottoming out on all the bumps.)

Well, it was on this trip that my rear tire totally wore through. It was on the return trip, and it wore out much more quickly than it should have due to the heavy load. My tire gave out in Worland, Wyoming—about halfway through the state but miles from any shop with a replacement tire for my Harley. After a long stretch of riding that morning, we had stopped to get a salad at a McDonalds. As Sharee and I pulled out of the parking lot, I knew something was seriously wrong, but we couldn't see the tire with the luggage draped all over the bike. As I hobbled the motorcycle over to the side of the road, it happened to be right in front of a U-Haul Truck Rental outlet. With no spare tire within 160 miles, I decided to rent one of only two U-Haul trucks remaining, gunned my Harley with a flat tire up the narrow loading ramp, tied it down inside the truck, and drove the rest of the way home to Utah —arriving safe and sound. Lessons learned? I always check my tires now before embarking on the day's ride, and whenever in doubt, I just put on a new tire. And no more heavy loads without taking the necessary precautions.

LETTING GO OF UNNECESSARY BAGGAGE

There are things that are definitely worth being concerned about. Yet there are other things in life that consume a tremendous about of time, energy and resources that don't really matter. They are the loads and burdens that are not really necessary to carry, but we often do anyway. As a life balance coach, I have also noticed that people worry about things (or people) they can't control. When they instead focus on what matters most, it's amazing how many things fall into line.

I remember a client who would come to our office, and the wife would constantly complain about how her husband would come home from work, plop down in the easy chair, kick off his shoes and read the newspaper. When he would get up and retire for the night, he would leave his shoes behind. This drove her crazy. She constantly complained about how he cluttered the living room and couldn't he somehow, someway, pick up his shoes and put them in the closet where they belonged. Then, he had a stroke and died. She came in as a widow about a year later to reassess her financial situation.

I asked, "How are you doing?" She said, "Not good. I have never been so lonely in my life." Then she confessed, "Do you know what I miss most about not having my husband? Not having his shoes lying about. Why was I making such a big deal of that for so many years?" With misty eyes she said, "I'd give anything to have one more night with his shoes cluttering my living room."

It's amazing how little things can stand in the way of us having a rich relationship. Life is way too short to get upset about things that really don't matter. I remember when we were first married, I would get perturbed at certain things Sharee did, and Sharee would get frustrated at things that I did. If she would leave the toothpaste tube cap off, I would get upset and constantly say, "Why can't you remember to put the cap back on the toothpaste?" Frankly, she doesn't even remember doing that. She'd watch me take a strand of floss and say, "Why do you need that much floss?" It was probably three or four inches longer than what she thought I needed, which only amounted to a few cents worth of extra floss a week.

When we were first married, we brought together two different family cultures, as many companionships do. We would have Thanksgiving dinner on certain years with Sharee's family, and other years with my family. I learned to adopt my personal attitude: Blessed are the flexible, for they shall not be bent out of shape. You see, when we had Thanksgiving dinner with my family and the time was set at noon, that meant we ate at noon and everyone was dressed up. It was a formal, on-time type of occasion. If Thanksgiving dinner was set at noon with Sharee's family, if we sat down and ate any time within four hours of noon, it was on-time. Many of her siblings would come in shorts or Levis and sweatshirts. That was new to me. But whether it was toothpaste caps and floss, or family gatherings, we have learned to roll with the punches and enjoy each of our families, regardless of the differences.

One of the other insights I've gained is that people often beat themselves up for things in the past, carrying the baggage around forever. The woulda's, shoulda's, coulda's can keep us trapped and our life off balance. Let's instead focus on what we *are* doing right; what we *did* accomplish, instead of on what's *not* going right in our lives. We can stay centered on the things that are positive, rather than negative; and we can let go of what we wish were happening. We have an acronym in our family that spells TEAM, which means Together, Everyone Achieves More. We want everyone to be a support to one another, so that when the loads are heavy, we can help lift the load from each other. Together, we are better.

THE IDEAL ME VS. THE REAL ME

One of my life coaches, Leo Weidner, years ago shared the following exercise with me. It came from a book that he wrote called "Achieving the Balance." He told me to take out a piece of paper and write down the basic areas of my life in the order that I would like to ideally live them in. For example, when I initially did this, I listed:

1. Spirituality
2. My role as a husband
3. Mental and emotional health
4. The type of father that I wanted to be
5. My business
6. My physical well-being
7. My church and community service
8. My professional endeavors
9. Financial health
10. Social life

After I listed my priorities, he told me to put away the piece of paper and live my life normally for a few weeks. Then I was to take out the paper after about three weeks and write down how I was actually living my life—the actual me. Here's how it broke down:

1. Financial health
2. My business
3. My professional endeavors
4. Church and community
5. Mental and emotional health
6. My role as a husband
7. Spirituality
8. My role as father
9. Physical well-being
10. Social life

It was a rude awakening. I had to ask myself why I had discrepancies. The honest answers to the why's reveal the parts in our lives that should be adjusted. I'm a visual person, so from that point forward, I began to color-code my time in six different colors. I did that by taking out a weekly calendar and dividing up a day from 5:00 am to midnight, in 30-minute time slots. On Sunday night I would look at my week and color in how I intended to spend my time in one of six colors:

- **Yellow** = spouse / partner time (because my wife is blonde)
- **Orange** = family time
- **Purple** = community and church service
- **Green** = what I do in my business in front of clients where I'm earning a living.
- **Red** = paperwork, administration, errands, e-mails, and the busy work of my profession.
- **Blue** = personal time (exercising, or doing something maybe just with my sons or my friends, golfing or whatever)

I would fill it out, and I could see visually how my week was going to go. Then every day, at noon, at dinner time, and before I went to bed, I took out those highlighters and I colored each 30-minute slot during the week of how I actually spent my time. The actual me didn't look anything like the intended me. It took six months before the one I filled out during the week began to mirror the one that I intended to a week before. When I mastered the art of being able to live the life I wanted to lead, my life got simpler, and my income doubled. That is the power behind having a vision and a focus of what is going right, especially when the load is heavy.

TRY THIS EXERCISE

As an Abundant Living Coach, I've helped our clients focus on all three dimensions of Authentic Wealth: financial, foundational and intellectual. It's been important to me to not only teach these principles, but to live them. And one of the best ways we've found to incorporate these values? With something you might like to try—it's an exercise based on what Dan Sullivan, my good friend and founder of The Strategic Coach, calls the R Factor and DOS Exercise. The R means Relationship. DOS represents Dangers, Opportunities and Strengths. It's become a favorite family activity during the holidays, and although at first it may not sound fun, it has opened a world of communication, growth, and yes, even fun, for myself and those I care about.

We do it with our children and grandchildren every year during the month of December. It's become not only one of the highlights of our Christmas season, but it is also a huge payday. We all get on the same page—in an abundant mindset—and cheer each other on for the goals we set for the New Year.

Here's how it works: For 15 or 20 minutes, every family member writes down what progress needs to be made with 10 relationships or areas in our lives for us to be happy. We write down a goal, or vision, for the following: 1) deity (God, or whatever your belief is in a higher power); 2) our spouse (or parents, for the children); 3) our children (or siblings, for the children); 4) extended family (or friends, for the children); 5) our physical health; 6) our finances/self-reliance; 7) intellectual milestones; 8) our business/job/school; 9) our church service; and 10) our community service.

Once we identify what has to have happened during the time period (e.g., the year 2015), then we identify the DOS. For dangers, we take the time to think through the road blocks, hindrances, or barriers that would prevent us from achieving these goals, and more important—how we will eliminate those dangers. When it comes to opportunities, we list the greatest opportunities that we need to seize in order to accomplish that vision. Finally, for strengths we list the greatest strengths or resources that we're going to draw from in order to accomplish the goals to seize a brighter future.

Let me illustrate. Say we set a goal to lose weight and get healthy. A Danger would be that we might end up having surgery or a heart attack, or are not "at ease" physically (which is what we called dis-eased). Another barrier might be that we don't think we have enough time (but the reality is, if we don't invest the time to exercise, we'll be forced to take the time recovering from the repercussions of not living a healthy lifestyle). Maybe some of the Opportunities would be to enroll with a trainer, or to take a yoga class, or to be accountable to a nutritionist. The Strengths or resources could be the professionals we can utilize and the books that we can read, thereby harnessing their support. Other resources might be to use a gym or a fitness center and others who have similar goals as a support group.

Or let's say you want to get your financial house in order. The Danger might be that you end up a year down the road still with consumer debt, or that you might outlive your money in retirement because taxes are going up dramatically; inflation will cut the purchasing power of the dollar in half every seven years (at the current rate of 10%), and market volatility continues in America. You should plan to eliminate those dangers. The Opportunities might be to refinance your home in a 60-year low interest rate, or to meet with a wealth architect that can help you optimize assets and minimize tax. The Strengths and resources are to read, study and utilize the best tools out there to do it.

Whatever the goal is, identify clearly where you want to be a year from now, and then get extremely clear on how to get there by eliminating the dangers, seizing the best opportunities, and harnessing the best strengths. This helps you go from a 55% chance of achieving your goal to up to 90% to 95% likelihood that you will achieve your brighter future.

FOUR KEYS TO A BRIGHTER FUTURE

As every year closes, it's a time of both reflection and planning for many of us. How do you approach the end of each year? Do you have a process for reviewing annual performance and setting goals for the coming year? Do you analyze the successes and setbacks, decide what can be done differently and define your strategies for the next year? Or ... do you tend to shoot more from the hip, heading into the future with a general "let's take it as it comes" approach?

In life, I have seen throughout my four decades of working with highly successful people, you are more likely to come out ahead when you head into the future with direction. And the best way to do that is by maintaining four key qualities: clarity, balance, focus and confidence.

Oft times people will ask, "Doug, what is it you do?" Now, I could answer that I have helped people plan for retirement for 40 years; that I'm an Abundant Living Coach; or that I'm a national speaker and bestselling author. Usually, however, I simply respond: "Well, we provide clarity, balance, focus, and confidence to individuals, families, businesses, industries, America, and the world."

Now, let me explain this. When people gain clarity, they have a clear vision of what matters most to them and what they're trying to accomplish. I've found that when people have absolute clarity about where they are and where they want to go with every aspect of their lives—finances, health, spirituality, relationships—they're energized, open to new ideas and strategies on how to get there. This brings profound hope for a brighter future and a sense of vibrancy. Essentially, clarity provides energy.

Let's look at balance. Imagine a car hurtling down the highway. At 65 miles per hour, if there's a wobble in even one of the tires, it will cause damage to the driving system and require more fuel to maintain speed. If you fix the wobble, however, you'll increase the car's efficiency, velocity and safety—and arrive at your destination with peace of mind. When you have balance in your life spiritually, physically, financially and with your relationships, you not only journey through life at a greater velocity, but you actually enjoy the ride!

When it comes to focus, too many people live their lives completely out of focus. They don't know how to prioritize and they struggle with what I call ADHD living—Attention to Daily Hiccups and Distractions. Rather than have a proactive approach to creating and pursuing their life's plan, they live moment to moment, paycheck to paycheck, problem to problem, entertainment to entertainment. They're always focusing on things they can't control or things that don't really matter. To live a fulfilling life, you have to determine what matters most and focus on those priorities that you have control over. This increases the accuracy with which you'll achieve your goal, your vision, and your future.

Now, let me stop right there to review. We've talked clarity, balance, and focus. If people looked at incorporating even clarity alone into their lives, they would have a about a 55% chance of being a happy, successful, captain-of-their-own-soul kind of person (versus meandering through life living vicariously through the Twitter feeds of movie stars recording what they're doing every second). So clarity will give them energy to move forward, right? And now if they were to add balance and take the wobble out of life, their chances go up to about 90% that they will be the determiner of their own happiness, avoiding the need for distractions and even self-medications like drugs and alcohol. And then, when they also add focus, that increases their odds to about 99%. What do all of these three bring? Clarity, balance and focus can't help but bring about the final ingredient for an abundant life: confidence.

Confidence attracts opportunities. Lack of confidence repels opportunities. When the DVD, "The Secret" was first released, while I didn't agree with everything it depicted (like the boy getting the bicycle without putting some skin in the game), I looked at my wife and I said, "That's no secret, that's been in the good book for millennia." If you exercise faith and confidence, you will attract opportunities. It's that simple.

And these are the simple keys to a brighter future: clarity, balance, focus, and confidence. They will help you eliminate the wobble, balance the load, and keep you upright (with full tires!), heading safely along your journey.

RETHINK YOUR THINKING

U: *How can YOU ...?*

- *Lighten your load?*
- *Balance your life better and handle the bumps with ease?*
- *Avoid worrying about things you can't control or that don't really matter at the end of the day?*
- *Prioritize your life and constantly assess what has to happen in every relationship?*
- *Maintain better clarity, balance, focus and confidence?*

F: How can you empower your close circle of FAMILY and FRIENDS to do the same—by being the best example of living a life of balance and giving them the gift of clarity?

O: How can you encourage OTHERS to do the same?

6 IT'S NOT ABOUT HOW LOUD THE NOISE IT'S ABOUT THE TONE

Roy:

We Harley riders are always concerned about the sound of the exhaust pipes. We adjust them and then swap them out for new ones and then adjust the new ones. The goal? Not too loud, not too quiet, but just right to be heard and recognized by all within hearing distance that another cool Harley is approaching.

As children of our Creator, we all are given our own voice. We use our voice to make ourselves heard, to connect with others, to share our lives … and depending on the situation or our attitude, the sound of our voice can be an outward expression of our inward desires or feelings or challenges.

Some of us are known by all to be too loud. Some of us are so soft that we are never noticed or acknowledged. Some of us can make beautiful music and some of us make music very ugly.

We spend all our time and effort working out the details of the sound of the pipes on our Harley, but do we take the time to step back and be aware of the sounds of our voice and the positive or negative effects that those sounds have on the people we love and the people we are trying to have a positive influence for good on? Do we make a conscious effort to monitor and control the volume and tone of our words in our attempts to send the message that we intend to be sending?

Maybe it's time for us all to take our ear plugs out and listen to the sounds coming from our own mouth and be introspective in the use of those sounds and how they affect our ability to win friends and influence those we love.

Doug's Take:

Each of the Harleys I have owned, as well as the Jeeps I've built, become an individual work of art. That's part of the excitement and intrigue of buying a stock vehicle and then gussying it up so it becomes one-of-a-kind. By the time I have my Harleys and Jeeps equipped and customized the way I want, I'm usually into the enhancements as much or more than the original purchase price of the stock vehicle from the dealer—although this process may be years in the making. So it is with our individual characters.

As Roy said, a distinct component that differentiates a Harley is its "sound." I personally like a deep "guttural" rich sound from my pipes (both on my bike and my own windpipe). It makes you unique. When with a large group of Harley riders on some of our trips, if there are several motorcycles ahead of me and Roy's is one of them, I can usually tell if it's Roy accelerating because I recognize the sound of his pipes. Many in our riding groups have said that they can recognize the distinct sound of my pipes within a short time of following behind me. I had a dear friend whose Harley had "Thunderheaders"—and it was impossible to mistake his bike—especially when he revved up.

As a public speaker, teacher, radio and TV show host and seminar presenter for more than 40 years, I estimate conservatively that I have spoken to public audiences for well in excess of 80,000 hours of my life. While traveling in some of the most remote areas in the world I have had numerous experiences of people that I've met who, when they hear my voice, exclaim, "I know that voice!" Last year we were in the Dominican Republic with Roy and Glenda on a humanitarian trip and 50 dental volunteers. While there we met an elderly couple from the United States who had lived on the island for about a year. Within two minutes, the man said, "Wait a minute, I recognize that voice. I heard you on the radio a year or so ago!"

Every one of us has our own unique voice. We should make it heard and recognizable—especially to those people we care about the most. I would recommend it be a voice that fosters soothing calmness and confidence, rather than one that exudes irritation and fear.

HOW DO WE COMMUNICATE?

As humans, how do we truly communicate?

- 55% of effective communication is body language
- 38% is the tone that you use
- Only 7% are the actual words

It's how you communicate with body language and tonality that makes all the difference. I love the T-shirt that shows how a subtle stroke of punctuation can change everything. It says:

Commas save lives.
Let's eat, Grandma
Let's eat Grandma

I remember listening to Zig Ziglar one time, and he said if a young man dating a young lady were to say, "When I look into your eyes, the wheels of time stand still," that would be considered poetic, romantic. But if you were to say, "Honey, you've got a face that would stop a clock," you would not score any points. You're basically saying the same things, but it's the way you say it that carries the meaning.

That is why I would much rather communicate a message by leaving a voicemail whenever possible, rather than sending e-mail. When I leave a voicemail, people can hear my tone. There are many times when I've written an e-mail, and when they answered it, depending upon the mood or attitude they chose to read into my message, they may have gotten defensive. When I followed up and realized they were offended, I repeated verbally what I said in the e-mail with the right tone, and it made all the difference in the world.

It's interesting how many people make assumptions that the way we give communication is the way that we love to receive communication. That is not always true. I like receiving e-mail, but I would much rather give communication via voicemail.

Also, timing is everything in communicating. For example, I would work all day long, and I just wanted to come home and have quiet time in the evening and relax. I'd been talking to adults all day as a financial strategist. I preferred to get up early, exercise, and talk about all kinds of things with my wife first thing in the morning. On the other hand, my wife had been talking with the kids all day. She was dying to have an adult conversation in the evening. She couldn't wait for me to come home to talk until the wee hours of the morning. It took us probably three decades of marriage to figure that one out.

The most important thing about communication is how your spouse, or other people close to you, like to handle stress. Often women simply want the men in their lives to listen, understand, and empathize. They don't want you to fix it. Men often assume that if their wife is expressing frustrations, she wants you to fix the situation. Men are quick at gearing up to reply, rather than listening. As soon as they get the opportunity, they jump in and tell their spouse what they need to do to correct the situation.

No matter our gender, we should all listen with our heart more than with our ears. I believe effective listening is one of the most important things we can learn the art of, which is much different than just hearing somebody out.

Sharee and I can get in the car and be driving to St. George, Utah, a road trip of about four to five hours. About two hours into the trip, Sharee will turn and say, "Doug, have you listened to a word I've said?" And I'll say, "Sure I have!" And she'll ask, "OK, what did I just say?" And I'll hum and haw, and not be able to tell her what she just expressed to me. This is often one of the breakdowns in communication between people that are very close to one another.

UPSET OR NOT? YOUR CHOICE

Much of communication isn't just on the part of the sender, it's also the receiver. One of my favorite sayings came from Germany, which translated into English says, "You can choose to be upset, but you're not obligated to be." It's amazing how many times we seem to feel obligated to be upset or to react, rather than responding calmly with understanding.

Mark Twain once said, "Forgiveness is the fragrance that the violet spreads upon the heel that crushed it." The word forgiveness means "for giving". You're "giving" something rather than "taking" offense. I have realized that most of the time when I may have taken offense at something, the person really didn't intend to offend me. I just didn't understand—or they didn't, and I chose to take offense.

I remember going to a wonderful lady's funeral. On her program was the quote, "She was never offended, because she never took offense." I realized that maybe 5% or 10% of the time, perhaps someone did intend to offend me, but if I simply thought, "Oh, they just don't understand," we all would have been better off. If they had walked in my shoes they would have never said that. So, I simply forgive them and avoid taking offense. (The upside? This often makes them angrier, because if they do mean to offend you and you don't take offense, it bothers them that you are not reacting with anger.)

One day, one of my dear friends, Keith, a professional counselor, was in a mental ward at a hospital walking down the hallway. From his blindside, a man attacked him, knocked him to the floor, cut him and gave him a nosebleed. As Keith got up and was ready to counterattack and retaliate, three nurses jumped over the nurse's station and announced, "Joe is having a seizure! Joe is having a seizure!" He instantly went from retaliation, anger and revenge to assistance and compassion. Isn't it interesting how we have the power in our mind to instantly change from anger to compassion?

One day when I was in a hurry, I stopped by my brother Sherm's office and asked if he would like to go get a quick hamburger and fries. I had about 30 minutes and we got in the car and I was talking a mile a minute. We got into a left-hand turning lane in Orem, Utah—one of the busiest intersections in the state. We were about the sixth car back waiting for the arrow to turn green to let the cars through. I knew the intersection well. It operated with a motion sensor. I knew that as long as cars began to move through the left-hand turning lane, it would let as many as 15 to 17 cars through the intersection before turning yellow. However, if it sensed no motion, it would immediately turn yellow assuming there were no cars waiting to turn.

Well, on this particular occasion, the lead car in the left-hand turning lane was not paying attention. As this was unfolding in front of me, I turned to my brother and said, "Some dumb idiot is not paying attention. And now we're going to have to ..." No sooner did I get those words out, when the lead car finally woke up. It was the only one that got through the intersection. And as the car came into full view, it was a cream colored Chevrolet Monte Carlo with a distinguished, gray-haired gentleman driving it. I looked at Sherm, and said, "And it's dad!" It was our father. My father was one of the gentlest men you could ever know. He would never intentionally cause irritation or anger. I instantly changed from "some dumb idiot" to "oh, I wonder what's on his mind? Let's catch up with him and see if we can get his attention and take him to lunch!" What was it that had me taking that dumb idiot to lunch? It was the perspective of the person that I knew, and I immediately had compassion for him.

WHY I DRIVE ANOTHER HOUR TO MY DENTIST

Often the tone we take with our customers—from verbal communication to follow-through on services—can impact our business. To test what level you are perceived by your best customers (be it a commercial business or the busy-ness of life—where the customers would include your children, grandchildren, Scouts, fellow church or community members, etc.), what would their response be if someone were to say, "Oh, I know (your name)! He, or she, is such an incredible person because ..." (and then what would they say about the kind of a professional person, father/mother, grandfather/grandmother, uncle/aunt, scout leader, that you are)?

For example, I'll use Roy's son, Chris, who is an incredible dentist that "did not fall far from the tree", following in his father's footsteps as a great dentist. If I were to just say, "Oh, I know Chris Hammond. He's a dentist." He would simply be perceived as a commodity—in other words, there are lots of dentists—he's just one of them.

If I said, "Oh I know Chris Hammond; he has the latest and greatest techniques and equipment. He uses the best lab for his work!" He is one rung up the ladder—providing unique products.

If I said, "Oh I know Chris Hammond; he not only has the latest and greatest, but provides exceptional service! His professionalism is unsurpassed! He: 1) is always on time, 2) finishes what he starts, 3) does what he says he going to do, and 4) always says please and thank you." (These happen to be the four "refer-ability" factors that Dan Sullivan teaches, as well.)

I have found very few building contractors who do those four things, and subsequently, they do not get referred by the people they build houses for. Very few general contractors are friends with the people they built houses for because of lacking those four professional traits. Unfortunately, the exceptional service level is the highest that most business people ever attain.

If I said, "Oh I know Chris Hammond! He is (all of the above), but it is such a unique experience when I visit him! He has a daily huddle with his staff and makes sure that a relationship manager is assigned to every patient. I feel so special every time I walk into his office." You see, he has a unique water wall in his entrance, and as soon as I walk in, one or more smiling people pleasantly greet me with a handshake and personal touch (as opposed to some receptionists I've encountered that are protected by a desk and who act like I'm an interruption of their work). Immediately they tell me my room is ready. (Yes, there is a room where patients can relax, where fruit and private-labeled bottled water is provided in abundance—but I've never needed to sit there.) Dr. Hammond chose to invest in more patient rooms than a bigger "waiting" room (because nobody likes to wait). I am always attended to with sincere interest. The assistant makes sure I am comfortable and visits with me about my family and all of the things that they took notes of from my previous visits. (They took time to dictate notes from the last visit—including everything about my family, children and the things going on.)

When Dr. Hammond walks in, he always brightens the room and makes me feel so comfortable about what we are going to do. He keeps me informed while he is working on me and reassures me that all is going beautifully. He and his team always check and re-check several times if I am comfortable or need anything. After explaining things to me, Dr. Hammond doesn't condescendingly ask, "Do you have any questions?" Rather, he gently asks, "What questions do you have?" This is a much different approach. It encourages you to ask your questions. He has special flavored mouthwash and a "goody" bag for me when I leave. I receive a monthly newsletter from him and constant invitations to special patient appreciation events. It is such a unique experience every time I visit him! But the real reason that I drive for an hour to get to my dentist, I'll illustrate through a true story about Doctors Roy and Chris Hammond.

People value a meaningful transformation the most. Doctors Roy and Chris Hammond built beautiful smiles for both Sharee and me that gave us tremendous confidence. But it goes deeper than that. In November of 2013, I was teaching an incredible audience for three days in a Clarity Experience at my educational institute. The third day was a Saturday morning. My wife and I had worked out at the gym early that morning, and we were arriving at our office to greet our audience for the final day. When we arrived, the doors were locked, as is typical on Saturday morning. My daughter was already in the office, greeting the audience and getting them seated. As my daughter came out the back entrance to hold the door open for us, my wife was carrying a protein shake and her iPad, as well as some other materials. I went to help her, but she said she was fine and told me to go hold the door, so our daughter Mailee could get back to the attendees.

I went to hold the door and then I heard a loud thud. I turned, and to my horror, saw that my sweet wife had tripped over an uneven part of the concrete sidewalk and landed teeth-first on the sidewalk, because her arms were full. She had just had her wonderful teeth finished with the most gorgeous smile from Dr. Hammond. I turned and realized her teeth were chipped on the sidewalk and she was bleeding profusely. She began sobbing in pain and frustration that the incredible work that Dr. Hammond had just finished was all broken to pieces in one severe fall.

I helped her in and had nothing on my mind but to help my wife receive some relief from her trauma. Within a few minutes, she even forgot falling, which was a signal that she had a concussion. She did know, however, that I needed to get in and greet my audience and begin teaching them. She said, "Doug, go in, do a 'split-second turn' and get back into the state of mind that you need to change some people's lives today".

She said, "I will call Dr. Hammond." I knew at that moment that she would be okay. She called Dr. Hammond. He was teeing off at a father and sons golf tournament with his two boys. She could hear him tell the other men and boys to play through while he took this emergency call. He offered compassion and empathy and said assuringly, "Sharee, you are going to be fine. Everything will be reconstructed and you will have just as gorgeous a smile, however the trauma and pain is going to be very difficult for the next few hours. Please take a picture with your iPhone, send it to me right now, let me assess it. Then, go down to the emergency room, get X-rayed, get prescriptions for pain, but it will probably not be necessary to do anything until later this evening at the earliest. We will begin to assess what needs to be done first thing as soon as the pain is under control." She did that. He called several times while on the golf course to check on her. He reached out and offered to drive to our home that evening. We live an hour away. We insisted that we wait and come see him first thing on Monday.

He arranged his schedule and put her as a top priority, restoring her teeth back to the gorgeous smile that she loved and appreciated. This is one of the reasons why we will travel one hour to go see Dr. Chris Hammond, because he has made a meaningful transformation in our lives. It is more about the tonality, the feeling, the meaningful transformation that has taken place. That's why we recommend him enthusiastically to others.

Ironically, amid working on this chapter, I was working out at the gym early one morning with Sharee—almost exactly one year after Sharee's falling episode. As I was doing an exercise with a kettle bell (lifting it up by the handle, then letting it go and catching it from underneath while squatting back to the ground again), I came down too fast and hit my two front teeth hard on the kettle bell. One tooth dislodged and broke at the bone; the other tooth was also severely hit and broke. Yes, I had just had my teeth completed into a wonderful new smile just a few months earlier. It was Monday morning 6:30 am. By 9:00 am, Dr. Chris Hammond and his staff made time and had my smile restored again and prepared me for the root canal that I would receive on Wednesday, scheduling the full restoration to be completed with two weeks. Both Doctors Roy and Chris Hammond called and checked on me several times to make sure I was OK.

It is not only our dentist that treats us so special. When I had my foot operated on, my podiatrist came with her daughter to our home to see how I was doing after surgery. She appreciated the kind of patient I was and how I treated her nurses. Sharee's had half of her liver removed, and the surgeon (who is chief of surgery at a large regional hospital) came to our home to check up on her. How often does that happen these days? It's all about the tone—of treating others as you would like to be treated. People will bend over backwards to return the kindness.

RETHINK YOUR THINKING

U: *How can YOU ...*

- *Communicate more effectively with the right tone?*
- *Master your emotions?*
- *Make a meaningful transformation by creating value for others?*

F: How can you empower your close circle of FAMILY and FRIENDS to do the same—by listening, answering softly and creating a meaningful transformation for them?

O: How can you support and encourage OTHERS with whom you work and serve to do the same?

7

RIDING AWAY FROM DANGER

Roy:

Over the years most of my miles on a bike have been in the U.S. or Canada—and largely in the western part of the U.S. In these areas, one of the greatest dangers you can face is a deer, elk, coyote or other wildlife jumping in front of the bike. It's usually just before, during, or after the hours of darkness, and they tend to leap from trees or bushes on the side of the road. With little to no warning you can be taking on an extra passenger while going 40-70 miles per hour. Not the kind of surprise guest you want.

When riding a motorcycle on a two-lane road, you generally want to ride in one of the two "tracks" made by the tires of four-wheeled vehicles. You could ride between those tracks, of course, but then you're in danger of hitting oil drips and debris on the road, which I normally avoid.

I prefer to stay as far away from danger as possible, so I normally choose the track that is closest to the center line of the two-lane road. Here I have a broader view and more reaction time should something suddenly spring onto the road. I also avoid riding in the dark or at dawn or dusk, again to avoid active wildlife—and because the dim light limits my vision.

When riding in the European Alps a few years back, my friends Graham and Donna made it clear to me that my "safe" position in the center wasn't so safe there. With sharp hairpin turns on narrow roads, I would be exposed to oncoming traffic crossing into my lane. This was an entirely new consideration of a source of danger. Since they had very little on those roads, I was encouraged to stay to the right near the shoulder, away from the center line. So that is where where I stayed.

Life has so many similarities. My father always told me that nothing good happens after midnight, so my curfew was 12:30 am. That gave me time to drop off my date at midnight and be home no later than 12:30 am. When I was given permission to go to a sleepover at a friend's home and Dad was not around to monitor the 12:30 rule, I soon discovered for myself that nothing good happens after midnight. (I guess it's the hard lessons learned by not keeping the rules that really makes an impression on our future actions.)

Now everyone may have a different idea as to what the dangers areas of life are. Parents and peers often don't agree. There may be friends who love to ride on the edge of the danger line, and they invite us to keep them company. Since we hate to miss out on some perceived excitement or thrill, we might join in as close to the edge or oncoming traffic as possible.

I know; I have been there. I have associated with those who always want to test the gray areas of life. There are those who rejoice in darkness because that is where their gray activities can take place with the least chance of detection. They entice us to join in on the fun, but they rarely mention the pitfalls.

But as life goes on, we make our wrong turns, have our falls and learn about the danger of riding in the dark. We grow wiser. We find that what might seem right for us at the time is not necessarily the best track for us. If we're open to counsel and advice from those who have traveled this same road, those who have fallen and learned from their mistakes, we can be better off. We can benefit from counselors, mentors, and loving partners as we travel the road of life. And we can realize that even though it may not look as thrilling, traveling in the safe zone can help us avoid injuries—and we still get to enjoy the view.

Doug's Take:

Roy and I have been involved in Harley tours of four to 14 days to many spectacular, scenic places including numerous national parks and monuments, as well as treks to Canada, the Pacific Coast, the Blue Ridge Parkway (in the Appalachians). We've even been fortunate enough to go as far as Bavaria, Tuscany and the south island of New Zealand. Some trips there are just a half a dozen bikes. But on others we've had in excess of 30 bikes.

When riding in groups, it is usually safest to ride in "staggered" formation—offset from each other—at a safe braking distance from the bike in front of you. Hence, if the motorcycle in front of you is riding in formation closest to the center line of a two-lane road, you're obliged to ride closer to the edge to increase the safety of the group. Of course, I find myself in that spot more often than not, because Roy likes to lead (I'm glad to let him—and I respect my elders). As you already know, he hugs the center line, so I ride staggered on the opposite side of the lane. I have learned to watch for debris and gravel that can be close to the shoulder.

I've learned for myself while riding, and living, to be aware of the dangers of getting too close to the edge. Chances are, sooner or later, that no matter how skilled we think we are at riding there, life can catch us unaware, and those dangers can turn to damage, discomfort or pain—maybe even our demise.

WHEN THE SHOULDER GIVES WAY

We have some dear friends who years ago had a fall family tradition—an outing to cut firewood to use in their wood burning fireplace. One year they were making their trek with their two little girls, one of whom was just a baby at the time. As they were coming down a mountain switchback road, they encountered another truck as they came around a bend. Rather than finding a place to pull over and allowing the other vehicle to pass, both drivers, acting "macho," thought they could handle passing each other. Their brother-in-law was driving the pickup; the father was riding in the back bed; and his wife was holding the baby in the front cab. (This was prior to child car seats being required for safety.)

Our friends' truck got too far on the edge onto the soft shoulder, when the cliff gave way and the pickup truck rolled down the hillside to a little valley below. The father fell out of the pickup on the first roll. He then watched in horror as his wife, little girls and brother-in-law rolled several times until he saw his little baby girl fly out of the cab window and land on the ground just as the pickup cab rolled on top of her.

Even though injured, he ran down the rocky hillside to the crash. With every bit of adrenaline that was rushing through his body, he physically lifted up the pickup truck and found his daughter had miraculously fallen into an indentation made by a gopher, uninjured between the dented cab and the ground. What a blessing! While they were grateful, the entire accident could have been prevented had they been more careful, hugged the center and not gotten so close to the edge.

A FENCE OR AMBULANCE

Sometimes people think that rules, regulations and laws infringe on one's free agency. But when one's choices may endanger another's life, such as driving under the influence, it is better that laws and restrictions are put in place that protect everyone—even ourselves—from danger. One of my favorite poems that illustrates this point is titled, *A Fence or an Ambulance* by Joseph Malins.

A Fence or an Ambulance
by Joseph Malins (1895)

'Twas a dangerous cliff, as they freely confessed,
though to walk near its crest was so pleasant;
but over its terrible edge there had slipped
a duke and full many a peasant.

So the people said something would have to be done,
but their projects did not at all tally;
some said, 'Put a fence 'round the edge of the cliff,'
some, 'An ambulance down in the valley.'

But the cry for the ambulance carried the day,
for it spread through the neighboring city;
a fence may be useful or not, it is true,
but each heart became full of pity
for those who slipped over the dangerous cliff;

And the dwellers in highway and alley
gave pounds and gave pence, not to put up a fence,
but an ambulance down in the valley.

'For the cliff is all right, if your careful,' they said,
'and if folks even slip and are dropping,
it isn't the slipping that hurts them so much
as the shock down below when they're stopping.'

So day after day, as these mishaps occurred,
quick forth would those rescuers sally
to pick up the victims who fell off the cliff,
with their ambulance down in the valley.

Then an old sage remarked: 'It's a marvel to me
that people give far more attention
to repairing results than to stopping the cause,
when they'd much better aim at prevention.

Let us stop at its source all this mischief,' cried he,
'come, neighbors and friends, let us rally;
if the cliff we will fence, we might almost dispense
with the ambulance down in the valley.'

DECIDE ... AND LET GO

It's interesting how many people choose not to make decisions. They have "decidephobia." But while they hem and haw, what they don't realize is they're putting off a brighter future. When we make a decision we are free to move forward, but when we avoid deciding, we often dwell in the past, or worse, keep repeating patterns expecting different results. Often when we find people not willing to decide, they experience chaos in their life.

I think it's interesting to note the word decide comes from the root word "cide," which actually means to kill off. (Homicide is the act of killing another human being. Suicide is the act of killing oneself. Pesticide is the act of killing pests.) When you decide, you're killing off the alternatives and taking steps toward (hopefully) a better path. "Choose" is a future-based word. We teach our children and grandchildren to decide to live a life of abundance versus scarcity, to always look forward to a happier future, rather than trying to change the past. Yes, we want to learn from our experiences, but we want to decide which part of the past gets to come along for the ride, and we leave the rest behind.

When I decided to marry Sharee over 40 years ago, basically, I "killed off" all other alternatives or considering other women in a romantic, intimate way. I think this is one of the reasons why we have been so happily married for more than 40 years.

One weekend, I was at a conference with about 60 "out-of-the-box-possibility-thinkers," being facilitated by Marshall Thurber. After a long day of discussion and learning, Marshall assigned us all to go back to our hotel room (it was 10 pm at that time) and read a white paper consisting of about 40 pages that Buckminster Fuller had written just prior to his passing. We were to come back the following morning at 8 am, prepared to discuss it as a group.

The next morning, the bulk of the group immediately got off track on a tangent and were arguing what Buckminster Fuller meant in his white paper when he said, "there's no evil in the world." Finally, Marshall looked at me and noticed I was not buying into the argument. He asked for my take on things.

I told them that Buckminster Fuller did not say that there was no evil in the world. Rather, he said that men and women do not come into this world inherently evil. Buckminster, (often called "Bucky"), was a Christian and believed we had an existence prior to earth life—being born of heavenly parents—to whom we return to live with after our sojourn during mortality. So as Wayne Dyer put it, we are spiritual beings trying to have human experiences on earth, rather than human beings trying to have spiritual experiences. But in that process, we make choices, commit mistakes, hurt ourselves and often hurt others. But we have the power anytime to learn from the past and choose a brighter future.

Marshall had taught me to use metaphors when explaining myself, so I shared that it's sort of like when you scuba dive. The human body is naturally buoyant—especially in salt water. If the ocean is calm and you just relax, you can snorkel for hours without sinking—just by breathing calmly—especially if you're wearing a dive suit. In order to descend below the surface, you must put on a weight belt. I can't descend unless I put on at least six to eight pounds of weight.

When a person goes through the scuba diving certification course, one of the drills that you perform again and again is to protect yourself in the event that you may have an emergency and run out of air in your tank. The first thing you do is drop your quick-release weight belt (which will immediately fall to the bottom of the ocean), and then you must constantly exhale no matter how little air you may think you have in your lungs. If you don't, your lungs may explode, which of course is fatal.

I compared that example to how we come to earth, pristine and good. But we all make mistakes and sometimes hurt ourselves and others. These weights that we carry may be regrets, laws we have broken, addictions, choices, transgressions or even sins in the spiritual sense. I believe that Bucky was saying that at any time, we all have the ability to recover, ask for forgiveness, make restitution, let it go and move on. We can avoid carrying the burden of our past mistakes with us the rest of our lives. As a Christian, Buckminster of course believed in casting the burden onto Christ so he can take the load. All of us, no matter what we may have done in the past, have the ability to correct our course, get away from the shoulder on the road, and drive in the safety of the center again.

THE SWING OR THE CLUBS?

Let's say you were going to be playing in a golf tournament and you had the choice of using a professional golfer's swing, someone like Phil Mickelson, or you could use his clubs. Which would you rather use?

This analogy applies to all aspects of life. With your family, I'm sure you've seen the difference with your children. When they learn true principles and are empowered to apply them (the swing), they're much more successful than when they simply mimic an activity (the clubs).

As for me, I'd prefer to have the swing rather than the clubs in every part of life. When planning for a brighter future, I'd like to have the knowledge of how to optimize my assets and live abundantly throughout my lifetime. And I'd rather leave behind the ability to swing, rather than leaving behind the golf clubs and trophies to my posterity. For Authentic Wealth that lasts, my children and grandchildren will need to be self-reliant for generations.

In this book, we may show you which club to use on certain occasions—like when your caddy recommends a sand wedge vs. a 7-iron or a driver—but our intention is not to get into the specifics too much, because the swing is most important.

Now, the swing involves learning and applying true principles. There's a difference between merely believing something and experiencing it—once you live it, it becomes a truth to you. So all of the principles that I'm sharing with you, I have experienced, and they are truth to me.

If you think about it, our lives are a sum total of wisdom gained from countless interactions with other people who have influenced us. I am grateful to the many mentors in my life who have shared proven strategies with me, and I've married concepts and developed original ones to help other people, as well.

So whether it's with your business, your family, or in planning for your own retirement, remember to focus on learning … and passing along … the swing. You'll be on course for a much more abundant future, thereby enjoying the "back nine" of life (your retirement years) without the stress of running out of resources while leaving behind a generational wealth system that fosters responsibility and accountability in your family. This kind of living leads to a safe journey, one where you're not thrown off by the hairpin turns or the emerging deer, because you're driving right down the center.

RETHINK YOUR THINKING

U: ***How can YOU ...?***

- *Stay in the "safety" zone of life and eliminate as many dangers as possible?*
- *"Kill off" old ways of thinking that do not generate true peace and happiness?*
- *Focus more on the swing or strategy, rather than the clubs or commodities in life?*

F: ***How can you empower your close circle of FAMILY and FRIENDS to do the same —deciding to live the life they want to lead, where happiness comes from within rather than through the accumulation of things?***

O: ***How can you encourage OTHERS with whom you work and serve to do the same?***

8 IN A DEEP CANYON, GETTING HELP IS MORE DIFFICULT

Roy:

A while back some of my younger children and grandchildren were looking at old photos. They were pointing out the phones, saying, "Hey, look at these wired phones, this is so crazy." Wow, how things change. When was the last time you picked up a phone with a cord attached? When was the last time you used a pay phone? Without the need for wires, our breadth and depth of communication has expanded beyond our wildest dreams. Now we can stay in constant communication with everyone in our lives.

But, the fact is, there are still plenty of dead spots where we find ourselves without a signal. In these zones, we can't place a call, and even more important, we can't reach out for help in case of emergency. When we're on a bike trip, as fate would have it, it always seems like the breakdowns occur in a deep canyon or distant area where there is no cell coverage. We feel lost and alone, and it can require a hike—or asking for help from other riders who come along—to get assistance.

Well, isn't life like that? We go along, enjoying our independent, smooth ride until we have a breakdown. We look around for help. If we've abandoned everyone during the easy times, the people around us tend to move on and abandon us. The canyon only seems to get deeper, and the far-back reaches of the cave darker.

This is the time we need to face up to reality, admit how and why we got there, get to a point of communication and ask for help. Sometimes it even requires asking for forgiveness and seeking support from friends and loved ones.

Now, in my mind, the most important partner we have in our quest for help is our Creator. The good news is there are no dead zones where we can't reach His listening ear. Even if we have times when, because of a path we've taken, we feel He has closed the lines of communication, this is not the reality of our relationship with our Creator. He has perfect worldwide channels of communication, and they're always open.

Hope is the spark of a new and better future. If we never lose hope, and we are always humble and willing to go to others (and most importantly to our Creator through prayer), we can always find a way out of the deepest canyons and caves of our lives.

Doug's Take:

One of our favorite areas to ride is in southern Utah. We have had numerous trips to Arches, Capitol Reef, Zion and Bryce Canyon National Parks—both by motorcycle and by SUV. One summer on a trip to Grand Gulch Primitive Area, Sharee and I, along with several of our adult children and some of our grandchildren, went on a hike that we were confident would be less than three hours. We had taken this hike a few times before, but it had been several years since our last excursion.

The hike involves walking on a mesa full of cedars. To get to our destination, it is absolutely imperative that we hug the edge of the mesa overlooking the Grand Gulch, or we could easily veer off on an entirely different arm of the gulch. Well, sure enough, we got over-confident and got lost—for several hours. We ran out of drinking water, because we had only brought with us about a half-day supply. It was hot. The little children were tired, worn out and hungry. We all became dehydrated. We were lost in the middle of the desert with no way to reach out for help or guidance. We didn't have a GPS at the time.

We finally were able to identify a spot called Salvation Knoll, which historically saved some lost settlers on Christmas Day in 1879. They climbed this knoll and could see the Blue Mountains to the northeast. It was also our salvation, because our camp was close to the knoll. In the end, what was supposed to be only a three-hour hiking excursion turned out to be a harrowing 12-hour journey before arriving back at our camp!

We were so grateful to be back safe. Sharee, being the concerned mother and grandmother she is, quickly prepared dinner for everyone. She neglected to re-hydrate herself in her effort to take care of the rest of us. The next day she was in severe pain and very sick. We rode back to Salt Lake City, arriving home late on a Saturday. The next morning, Sharee ended up being rushed to the hospital in critical condition and was in intensive care for a couple of days with her life hanging in the balance. Her liver and pancreas had nearly shut down. Her physician said that it was a miracle that she was able to pull out of it—she had come very close to checking out.

We were not aware of the dangerous circumstances we were in when we were caught in a "deep canyon"—not just in southern Utah, but the deep canyon Sharee was in with her vital organs suffering from severe dehydration.

As Sharee and I exercise and hike together now, we always make sure that we have more than enough water and nutrition to sustain us, especially in the event we get delayed or stuck somewhere. I have often taught: It's a lot better to have access to resources and not need them, than to need them and not be able to get them, just like it's a lot better to have insurance and not need it than to need it and not be able to get it. It seems whenever we have given in and taken the spare tire, tool box, extra oil, or other emergency supplies out of our vehicles to make room for other unnecessary items, we end up regretting it.

KASH IN

Life is meant to provide us experiences, and we're meant to learn from them. There is no guarantee that it is always going to be wonderful. But I have learned to invest the time every day in cultivating KASH, so that when I feel like I've entered into a deep canyon in life, I can reach out and draw on strengths.

KASH is an acronym we use with our clients and family that means **K**nowledge, **A**ttitudes, **S**kills and **H**abits. I have developed rituals that help me accumulate KASH. I have realized it doesn't *take* time to do the following daily activities, it actually *saves* time as I invest in a more productive life.

First, I make it a point to read every day from good books, and some of my favorite reading is in the scriptures. I then meditate, ponder and pray. I write down positive accomplishments from the previous day and visualize positive accomplishments for the new day. I repeat affirmations about my values and what I believe—the kind of life I want to lead.

I exercise everyday—usually for at least one hour. I personally enjoy doing cardio workouts at least three days per week, and my wife and I work out with a trainer two to three days per week at a fitness center. (I'll explain more about our exercise routines in a later chapter.)

And, finally I love to write my goals—my vision for a brighter future—as well as my feelings. I especially enjoy writing down at least five things I'm grateful for.

As I mentioned, these habits help me KASH in the support, knowledge and comfort I need during challenging times, ensuring I'm not stuck without a lifeline in the valleys of life.

GOING NO-TECH

While we're focusing on what happens when you find yourself cut off from communication in life's canyons, there are also times when it might be nice, literally, to cut ourselves off from communication—going no-tech. On purpose. Yes. Without cell service or the Internet.

It's interesting how easy it is for us to get engrossed in media and technology, with our phones and tablets attached like an umbilical cord. When I travel the U.S. and globe for speaking engagements, I'll often look around on trains, buses, airline terminals and see at least 80% of the people staring at their handheld device, connecting to the world via the Internet. I've even noticed when I go to ask a question at a store, the employees are killing time by texting and staring at their tablets.

It was amusing to me the other day when I was reading the Old Testament, in Chapter 3 of the Book of Isaiah, something jumped out at me that I had never noticed before. Isaiah is prophesying about what will take place in the last days, saying that people will be caught up in their changeable suits of apparel, their headbands, their earrings, and their ornaments, chains, bracelets, rings, nose jewels and their tablets. Before, I never could figure out what he meant. Now, I understand.

We sometimes need to just get back to good old-fashioned communication with one another. Our family celebrates Grandpa's Camp, where Sharee and I set aside six days every summer for the grandchildren to come. The first two days, the grandchildren ages 12 and up stay (without their parents), and we share conversations and experience camping and high adventure. We talk about those things that are on teenagers' minds.

Then the next two days, the kids ages 4 and up come join them. The grandchildren teach each other principles. For example, last year, all of the grandchildren taught their cousins about what it meant to put on the whole armor of God, as found in the New Testament, the Book of Ephesians. They also teach each other skills, and we enjoy arts and crafts.

The final two days of Grandpa's Camp, the parents bring the toddlers to join in, and the children all share what they learned. This is powerful in that we do not allow any technology on this campout. They must leave their smart phones and their tablets home.

In everyday life, I know a lot of families that have a technology drawer. Everyone—children AND mom AND dad put their cell phones, their iPads, and their iTouches in the technology drawer, and they all gather around for family dinner and conversation, without the distraction of their devices. It changes everything.

I am fortunate to belong to an incredible group of individuals, known as the Genius Network Mastermind. It is facilitated by Joe Polish, one of the most brilliant connectors of people on the planet. We have an annual conference every year in which we meet for two days. One of my associates there enjoyed an entire summer with his son with absolutely no technology. They had a summer experience in the mountains in Alaska. He admitted that the first few days, he thought his son was going to go nuts without communicating with his friends. By the end of the summer, his son had read over 300,000 pages in books; they had had more in-depth father and son conversations than they had in years; and it all happened by getting rid of the technology for the summer.

One of the greatest pieces of advice that Sharee and I are extremely grateful for was to keep the technology and the phones out of the bedroom, including the TV and the DVD player. We have strived to always keep television and even our cell phones out of the bedroom as much as possible, and this allows for in-depth conversations that have dramatically enhanced our relationship.

It's without the crutch of our communication devices that sometimes we communicate even better, in real time, with the people really around us. And that connection is what can save us from the canyons, help us find our way through any situation, and enable us to continue our journey safely.

AVOID GETTING STUCK IN A DEEP CANYON

One of the most common questions I get asked is, "Doug, when something bad happens to me, how can I bounce back and land on my feet again quickly, so I don't get stuck in a rut?" You see, it's not that we can avoid entering deep canyons when we go on a Harley ride, but we make sure that we know how to reach out for help in difficult circumstances. We understand it's about being proactive rather than staying stuck in the canyon.

Here's one of the simplest ways of bouncing back no matter how much may go wrong on any given day in your life—where you feel like you're just on a losing streak in life. Change your mind and get on a winning streak!

First, consider where your focus is. Do you tend to look backward, mulling over the successes and setbacks, achievements and losses of the past? Or do you look so far down the road that you're living for the distant future? What if instead you focused, literally, on today and tomorrow? That's all: the day you just experienced, and the day you'll wake up to tomorrow. And what if we avoided beating ourselves up? My friend, Dan Sullivan recommends we simply measure ourselves by what we accomplished today, and that we set goals for what we hope to accomplish tomorrow.

He points out the easiest way to do this is by taking your journal, iPad or smart phone and writing at the top: Today. Under that header, write down three "wins" for the day—positive things you accomplished that were a success. Then write another header: Tomorrow. Under that, jot down three wins you hope to have tomorrow.

You may be wondering what kinds of actions qualify as a win. That is completely up to you. It may be getting your hour in at the gym, resolving a conflict with your spouse, closing the deal with the new client, or choosing salad over the pastrami burger. Whatever constitutes a step forward toward your vision of who you are and who you want to be—that is a win.

Dan has been doing this for 17 years without missing a day. I myself have made it a regular habit for quite a while. It may seem simple, but I can attest, it is very, very powerful.

No matter what happens, even if something negative interrupts my progress that day, I still think of three positive accomplishments that happened during the day. After I write those down, I write down the three wins that I hope to have for tomorrow. I do this in my journal, and I also use a free app called "WinStreak" that Dan Sullivan created for any smart phone or iPad.

Now when tomorrow comes, if I didn't accomplish the three wins I set out for myself, I don't torture myself over it. I just focus on three things I did get accomplished. By doing this, I'm seeing myself as having a winning streak. It's very motivating because if you're going to play the game of life, do you want to create a situation where you're always losing, or do you want to be winning?

The key is to get in the habit of focusing primarily on the positive and staying on your personal winning streak in life.

I encourage you to download the WinStreak app for your smart phone or iPad (or you use your journal), and test out this approach for at least two weeks. Watch how it makes you feel, and how it helps you go from success to success. You will not stay stuck in any canyon of despair for very long.

Ralph Waldo Emerson has said, "Write it on your heart that every day is the best day in the year." By focusing on the positives of today and setting yourself up for the same perspective tomorrow, you can celebrate life each day. And when you do, life, work, family, finances—everything—contributes to a beautiful life you're leading. And that definitely makes it all worth waking up to with a smile—a genuine, authentic, from-the-heart grin every morning. And THAT'S how you can get out of any deep canyon in life.

RETHINK YOUR THINKING

***U:** How can YOU ...*

- *Accumulate more KASH (Knowledge, Attitudes, Skills and Habits) to get on a WinStreak?*
- *Spend less time consumed with technology?*
- *Invest more time communicating one-on-one with others?*

***F:** How can you empower your close circle of FAMILY and FRIENDS to do the same?*

***O:** How can you encourage OTHERS with whom you work and serve to do the same?*

9

WHEN YOUR VOLTAGE REGULATOR WANES, YOUR BATTERY DRAINS

Roy:

Our Harleys have components of the electrical system that all need to be working in sync for the bike to give power to the spark plug, which provides the source of combustion that fuels the movement of the bike. If any of these components deteriorate, the entire system fails. You can have one little bad spark plug, and the bike quits.

This happened to my son-in-law on a long journey we were taking up into northern Canada several years ago. After trying to decide why his bike was running so poorly, always difficult to start, we finally took the spark plug out of another bike and tried it in his, and all was well.

On another occasion, one of my sons' had his bike quit, and it would not even turn over. To test it, we took the battery out of another bike, put it in his, and he was in business. We went into town and got him a new battery.

On a return trip from Sturgis, my son-in-law was on a brand new bike when it started to lose power. We struggled to find the problem. The spark plug was perfect and new. The battery was new and had a good charge. We finally discovered that the wire cable connecting the battery to the electrical operating system had a break in it. We cut the wire, made a splice and were on our way.

My most recent learning experience was with the bike my brother-in-law, Doug, was riding on a trip to Sturgis. As the trip started out of Salt Lake City, his bike began to act up. It would be fine, but then the generator charging light would come on … and then it would be fine again. With no place to go for help, we decided we needed to make our best shot at continuing until we could get closer to a shop. As we pulled into the parking lot at a canyon in Yellowstone National Park, the bike totally quit. The battery was completely dead. I contacted a dealer about a two hours' drive away and headed out to get a new battery. After making the trip there and back on my bike, it was well past time for bed. We were fortunate enough to get a room in the park.

The next morning we installed the new battery thinking all would be well. Only 10 or 15 miles down the road, the red light indicating the battery was failing came on again. By the time we reached Cody, Wyoming, the new battery was now dead, and we loaded the bike into a U-Haul truck so Doug and Sharee could drive it to the repair shop. The shop explained the factory had sent out a recall notice a few years back concerning the need to replace a faulty voltage regulator, but Doug had not received it and had no idea. With the replacement of the voltage regulator and another new battery, Doug and Sharee were on their way with no further delay to catch up with the rest of the group who had arrived at Mount Rushmore earlier that day.

Well, what does all of this have to do with life? As I see it, we have two main operating systems in our journey. There is our physical well-being, and there is our spiritual well-being. Both of these systems have several components that all need to be functioning in sync, or the system begins to shut down.

No matter how invincible we think we are, we need to remind ourselves that this is the one and only physical body we will get, and we need to do all in our power to keep it in good condition so it will carry us throughout life's mission. There are times we need to evaluate our care of our physical bodies, and perhaps even seek medical help.

Our spiritual system, in my opinion, is more complex. A slow deterioration can take place as we move along, inch by inch, mile by mile, down a path that we didn't even intend to be on. Sometimes there is a red warning light, but we say to ourselves that we have no choice but to go on because there is no help available. My life experiences tell me that there is always help available. We are never in the middle of Yellowstone National Park with no mechanics and no new batteries. We need to perform a diagnostic on our lives, reach out for love and support from loved ones, and seek help from our Creator through prayer.

In times like these, we need to say to ourselves, "If it is going to be, it is now up to me. No one else can do this for me. My battery is drained. I am going to clean up each component of my system and get back on the road to happiness."

Doug's Take:

On the trip to Sturgis that Roy just described, Sharee and I gained additional insights from that experience. You see, without having received the recall notice on my voltage regulator, I was not aware of the imminent failure. My annual maintenance visits for my motorcycle could have detected it had the service shop looked up pending recalls. While we could get frustrated and waste time blaming, justifying or operating in shame as I'll explain in Chapter 11, we just accepted the setback and did what we needed to fix the problem. It's only when we take responsibility and accountability that we move forward and progress in life—and then we can enjoy the ride.

Another takeaway? Roy immediately was able to contact a shop and secure a new battery—which we thought would solve the problem. It required extra effort on his part as he sent the rest of the group on their way to Red Lodge, Montana, as scheduled for the night, while he went to fetch me a new battery in another direction. Roy, Glenda, Sharee and I enjoyed the diversion and made the best of the delay with a night's stay in Yellowstone. Even though the next day I found myself loading my Harley onto a U-Haul to drive from Cody, Wyoming, to Red Lodge, Montana, Sharee and I made the most of the continued diversion. While the rest of the group traveled to Mt. Rushmore that day, Sharee and I hung out in Red Lodge and enjoyed a half-day while we waiting for our voltage regulator to be delivered to a drug store address. We were also prepared to stay in case we encountered more delays, but by early afternoon, Sharee and I were on our way. We rolled into Keystone, South Dakota, at about 10 pm, safe and sound. Yep, another I Remember When memory to add to our collection.

So now you know that I've had two breakdowns on Sturgis trips that have resulted in loading my Harley into a U-Haul truck and towing it to the nearest service center. I'm grateful for the positive outcome on both occasions. On future trips do we just schedule all pit stops in towns where there are truck rental outlets? Prevention, when possible, is far better than curing the problem.

What about when our own personal voltage regulators are in danger of an impending failure? What happens when we go, go, go and get burned out in life because our internal regulator is not able to maintain a fast pace—especially when we are "shorting out" in different parts of our life? Indeed our energy levels can and will drain and may leave us with a major breakdown, even stranded on a lonely path with very few resources to get us back going again. It's important to maintain our systems in life so we can keep on keeping on.

YOU CAN ALWAYS TELL WHERE SOMEBODY'S AT...

If you're thinking of heading somewhere you've never been before, here's a question for you: "What's the most important piece of information that you need to know?" Usually people blurt out, "Well, where I'm going or how to get there." Wrong. If you own a GPS, you'll know that's not the first bit of information it acquires. Your global positioning system uses triangulation to hone in on three satellites out of about 24 to 32 that orbit this earth at any given time to pinpoint your exact location. In fact, it can tell within two square feet where you are standing on planet Earth. You see, it doesn't care at first where you're going. It wants to know where you are.

Once your GPS has located you, you can program where you want to go, and it will show you all kinds of routes to get there ... you can choose from the scenic route, the by-ways, or the freeways. It can also point out where to refuel your car—and yourself on the way.

Over my 40-plus years as a financial strategist and Abundant Living Coach, people have asked me, "Doug, if you had your druthers, what would you rather do?" And, I enthusiastically respond, "I like to be the OnStar button on people's dashboard of life." In order to do that, I first help people get extremely clear on where they are in their lives and where they want to go; then I show them the best ways to get to their desired destination and live the abundant life they want to lead.

As I mentioned, I've been blessed in my lifetime to work with some the nation's leading experts, to learn from them, and to develop some of the best strategies and tools for arriving at our desired destinations. I love helping people transform their lives, find empowerment, and enjoy brighter futures. Marshall Thurber once told me, "Doug, you can always tell where somebody's at by where they're at." So simple, but so true.

I can usually look at someone's tax return or six numbers on their financial statement and tell where they are financially; how much of a fortune they're missing out on by what they're doing or not doing; what they think they know; and obviously what they don't know. (The fact is, you don't know what you don't know—because you can't be aware of something you're not aware of.)

Just the same, you can always tell where somebody is physically, mentally, spiritually, financially. And as Dan Sullivan says, "All progress begins by telling the truth." I think it is imperative for us to be fiscally and physically prepared for emergencies in life, so that we will be prepared for those times with unanticipated headwinds, and you need to draw on that extra fuel—as we will illustrate in the next chapter. It's like providing a GPS for one's soul, so that when your life's generator of true peace and abundance wanes, your energy and zest for living doesn't drain. This is about YOU—how YOU can have the most incredible, amazing future possible!

SHAPING UP

Marshall Thurber told me one day, "Different isn't always better, but better is always different." One of the incredible truths that I have learned is that we often try to pull off a transformation financially, physically, spiritually, or intellectually, without incurring any pain or discomfort. When we try to achieve something without incurring any pain or discomfort, we usually go back to our old ways. We don't lose weight. We don't change our eating habits. We don't exercise. We don't change spiritually. We criticize other people and think that they're hypocritical when we don't even see the hypocrisy in ourselves. Many times we try to change intellectually, but we say: I'm too old to start playing the piano now or to study, or to get an educational degree. These are all just excuses.

I have found that I only progress when I get out of my comfort zone, as explained in Chapter 1. That is where the magic happens. By age 55, I had pretty much taken my health for granted. I was one of very few males in my extended family that had not had some type of difficulty with heart problems or had bypass surgery. I bought into the thought that if my cholesterol was low, I was home free. My cholesterol had never been over 119. When I got checked out, I found out that my heart was working like that of an 80-year old, and I was only 55. I had to make a change. I had to do something different.

I was active as a skier; I played racquetball; but I really wasn't as healthy as I knew I needed to be. I never wanted to run. But, knowing that I weighed 193 pounds at six-feet tall, even though that was average for my age, I didn't want to be average. The average 60-year old male has a life expectancy of 22.6 years in America if they do not use tobacco. I wanted to beat those odds.

Now, God is going to take you when He takes you. But to increase the likelihood that I would have a longer life expectancy, I followed ten simple steps that Dr. Mark Hyman gave in his 10-minute talk at the Genius Network Mastermind meeting in New York a few years ago. He spoke on how you can dramatically increase your chances to have a life expectancy that exceeds age 100. Many people will not follow these tips because they may seem painful.

Long story short, Sharee and I began to exercise. I can do lots of things now, and I'm in better shape than I've been my entire life. In fact my wife and I box (not each other, but we box punching bags) and burn about 800 – 1,000 calories in an hour. We can crank out several sets of push-ups, climb a rope primarily with upper body strength, and do other things that we have not done since high school.

Was it painful to start running? Yes, I had never seen runners with smiles on their faces. They always seemed to have grimaces on their faces. But on a family vacation in 2005 we started running. The first 10 to 17 days were pretty miserable, but then it became very enjoyable. Pretty soon I did not want to miss out on that oxygenation and exhilaration. I thought clearer throughout my day, and I had more energy. I realized it was now *more* painful to go back to my old lifestyle once I had made the transformation. So, I now run on the average three times a week—not long distances, maybe three to five miles—but it's painful if I don't exercise.

Now, I did not lose weight even though I was in great shape. So, we met with a top nutritionist and we learned some things we never learned in health classes in school. We began to eat smaller portions more often—six meals a day and we changed the ratio of our fuel to 50 – 60% the right kinds of low glycemic carbs, 30 – 40% the right kinds of lean protein and 10 – 20 % the right kind of fats. Was this painful to change? Yes, but once we had made the change, the weight came off, and my wife and I lost thirty pounds each in ninety days. For the last four years, we have not gained weight between Halloween and New Year's Day, when most Americans gain, on the average, 12 pounds. Many Americans do this and then they only take off 10 of the 12 pounds in January, and thirty years down the road they're sixty pounds overweight ... and they wonder what happened.

The third truth was to understand the need for cleansing. So, after going through an intensive 11-day cleanse to rid our bodies of the toxins we all accumulate with our lifestyles and the environment we live in, we enjoyed the strategic benefits of losing weight and reversing the aging process, making our skin, arteries and organs more pliable and "elastic." We now maintain our physical engines by taking two ounces of cleanse in the morning and also in the evening.

The point is, because we learned about how to maintain a healthy lifestyle, our physicians agree that we've increased our life expectancy dramatically. All we did was learn true principles and implement them. Was it painful? Yes. It was different, and different was better. Once we made the changes, we now enjoy all kinds of opportunities with increased energy. I assure you, as you embrace the pain and discomfort, you will reach destinations you never dreamed possible for yourself.

Besides having a generator for your spiritual and physical needs, I can't help but take a moment and use this metaphor as it relates to one's financial needs, because generating all three dimensions of Authentic Wealth is what I've been passionate about helping people with my entire life.

BATTERY VS. GENERATOR

Let's review what Roy articulated. What is the difference between a battery and a generator? It doesn't take an electrical engineer to tell us that a battery provides power for all kinds of electronics, but its ability to provide that power is limited. If it's your car battery, it may help keep your vehicle going for a few years before it's time to replace it. But if it's your phone battery (and it's like mine!), it may not even make it until the end of the day before you have to recharge it. A generator, on the other hand, can provide power for a much longer span of time and for much bigger needs. It simply needs the right fuel (typically some type of gas), and you can use a generator's power for all kinds of things, from providing electricity for big machinery, all the way up to an entire movie set or hospital.

You know, in the 40-plus years that I've been a financial and retirement planning specialist, I've noticed that a lot of financial advisers unfortunately have a "battery mentality" when it comes to their clients' retirement. (It's not necessarily their fault—it's how traditional financial education goes.) Essentially, they follow conventional wisdom, which tells you to approach your future by "charging up your retirement battery" just enough that you'll have funds to last as long as you do (crossing fingers that it won't die before you do).

Many in the financial services industry have this 4-volt mindset, because they use the industry standard 4% Rule. The 4% Rule is used to determine the amount of funds you should be able to withdraw from your retirement account each year. The idea is the 4% Rule helps provide a steady flow of retirement income while keeping your account balance sufficient for withdrawals for the years to come based on your life expectancy. Bottom line: They don't want you to take out any more than 4% a year or else you will outlive your money.

But if we look at what that means in real-world terms, you would need to have a nest egg of $1,250,000 to generate (after tax) a net spendable income of $3,000 a month, which is $36,000 a year. Well, I don't know if you're like I am, but I wouldn't want to accumulate $1,250,000 just to have a measly three grand a month to buy gas, groceries, prescriptions, golf green fees, and so forth. Especially when you factor in other conditions that can cause a drain on your battery:

- Taxes
- Inflation
- Market volatility

I would rather have a generator that never runs out, the kind that provides twice the voltage or even ten volts! Think about it—what if that $1,250,000 nest egg were generating $100,000 to $125,000 a year of tax-free income? Personally, I use powerful wealth generators that generate predictable tax-free income where my money is linked to inflation—so inflation helps me—it doesn't hinder me, and I am protected from loss when the economy or markets are down. My nest egg doesn't run out of power; it generates tax-free income for life and will continue on for many generations.

That is why I call it "generational wealth," because you'll never outlive your money, and it will pass on to your spouse, your children and your grandchildren into perpetuity. So why not look at ways to generate wealth into perpetuity, versus creating a limited supply?

What would that kind of ongoing wealth mean for you and your family? When you look at your children and grandchildren, wouldn't you rather leave something behind that can continue to grow and bless their lives, encouraging them to share in the "Family Bank" in a way that they can use money for college, to start a business, philanthropic causes, go on to generate more wealth, and feed abundance back into the family fund?

I will give fair warning, this is the kind of wealth that takes proper research, planning and execution. It takes more energy and purposeful living than just following the crowd's battery mentality. But it's also the kind of Authentic Wealth that generates true abundance not only for your retirement years, but also for your family's future. And that is worth it!

Whether it's your physical well-being, your spiritual life, or your financial health, making sure you have everything in working order—at all times in life—is critical for a smooth ride. Luckily even if we let things fall out of condition, we can take ourselves to the shop, fix things up, and get back on the road to enjoy the journey.

RETHINK YOUR THINKING

U: *How can YOU ...?*

- *Better prepare yourself so that in every area of your life—physically, financially, emotionally, spiritually, and socially—gain clarity on where you're at?*
- *Determine where you want to go and how to get there?*
- *Use the resulting energy and power to sustain yourself through the end of your life "ride?"*

F: How can you empower your close circle of FAMILY and FRIENDS to do the same— understanding where they are at and where they want to go in life to generate Authentic Wealth?

O: How can you encourage OTHERS with whom you work and serve to do the same?

10 HOW MUCH GAS IS IN YOUR TANK?

Roy:

All of my Harleys have been reliable to travel around 45 miles on a gallon of gas. Over the many years of riding, I have run out of gas on two occasions. These two experiences have increased my wisdom concerning the variables of the ride that can affect that reliability.

Yes, you do use more gas going uphill, but in general, the uphill and the downhill miles pretty much average out so that this becomes a non-issue. My experience tells me that the real issue is wind. If you are riding into a strong headwind for extended periods of time, your gas consumption can and will increase significantly. Let me share how I learned my lessons.

Several years ago I was on a road trip across Highway 50, the loneliest highway in America, with a group of guys on our way to Reno, Nevada. On this stretch of road there are very few gas stations. The rule is you never pass one without filling up. I was riding at the back of the group. My bike holds five gallons of gas, and so at 45 miles per gallon, I can go 225 miles. The other riders had six-gallon tanks on their touring bikes. The stretch between gas stations was 180 miles.

We were heading west toward Reno into a strong headwind, and after about 175 miles from filling up, my bike quit and I was completely out of gas. The group had disappeared, and I was on the side of the road alone. I could see a small trailer park about one mile down the road, so I started off on foot. I met up with a guy there mowing the grass and asked him for help. We jumped into his pickup truck with a can of gas and headed back to my bike. He lit up his cigarette as we were driving and then pulled in behind my bike. He jumped out, grabbed his can of gas, went to my bike and started to pour the gas into the tank. Because of the strong wind, gas was splashing everywhere and he still had his cigarette in his mouth. Well, I just kept my distance and said a prayer. I gave him $20, and he was on his way with the cigarette still burning. I was able to catch up with the rest of the group, with my lesson on the effects of a strong headwind learned.

Well, many times in life it seems we don't always remember the lessons we learned earlier in life. My wife and I were headed home from Sturgis out of South Dakota, down through Wyoming to Cheyenne. I passed what I later realized was the last gas available before Cheyenne and headed into a strong headwind, thinking all would be well. We ended up coasting and pushing the bike up to the front of a small farmhouse that had two large gas tanks at the side of the house.

I knocked on the door and out came a woman who had to be at least 99 years old. She came out in her bathrobe to pump gas for us. She first tried to put in diesel fuel, but I interrupted that just in time. She then moved to the other tank and got some regular gas in the bike. No one else was around as far as I could see. I gave her a $2 bill that I often carried in my wallet along with a twenty-dollar bill. She looked at the $2 bill and said, "Young man, I have not seen one of these since I was in Vegas. Thank you!" Well, all is well that ends well, but I know the rule, three strikes and you are out. I have two, and I hope I am wiser in the future!

Don't you think life is like this in many ways? First, do we have to learn a hard lesson more than one time? Do we forget our mistakes and repeat them over and over again? Do we keep doing the same thing over and over again thinking that we will get different results? This is a very foolish way to live our lives.

Another lesson to be learned: We can do anything in life, but we cannot do everything. Our Creator will not give us a challenge that we cannot bear with His help.

But, when we commit ourselves to more than our health and energy can endure, where we make promises we cannot keep, we are going to find ourselves out of gas on the side of the road. It is better to do a few things really well than to do a whole lot of things mediocrely.

We all have different levels of endurance, different capacities in our gas tank and our responsibility is to understand how far that tank can carry us and always try to put the important things of life before the urgent. If we don't make a conscious effort to do this, the urgencies of life will drain our time and fuel, and we will never get around to the important things. We are then in danger of leaving this life with totally unacceptable regrets.

Doug's Take:

Fortunately, I have never run out of gas on my Harley—even though I've come awful close on several occasions. I'll admit that I *have* run out of gas plenty of times while operating cars, Jeeps, boats, jet skis, ATVs and even one time while piloting an airplane (which story I'll relate at the end of this chapter).

What about being more aware of how much gas or energy we have to travel through life with physically, emotionally, mentally, socially, financially and spiritually? Life is full of unexpected headwinds and uphill drives that will challenge our endurance. One of my favorite lines from the movie, *Forest Gump,* is "Life is like a box of chocolates—you never know what you're going to get!" An anonymous writer once said, "If you want God to chuckle, tell Him what you're going to do the rest of your life!" I have been blessed to learn some very significant exercises that keep the gas tank of my soul and body at or near full and able to get me through the rough times.

TRY THIS EXERCISE

As anyone who has seen significant success knows, true progress hinges on creating and maintaining a vision of where you want to go, providing a map for how to get there, and establishing accountability for reaching the steps along the way.

Whether you're leading a team at work, or heading a growing extended family at home (with in-laws and grandchildren joining the crew), here's an exercise you may find useful … the What's It Worth activity.

What's It Worth is an exercise I do with my team at work .. and I've even found it valuable with my family (which for me does indeed include grandchildren), Scout groups I've worked with, and more. It helps us ensure we don't run out of gas or get burned out in real life.

The activity was inspired by my friend, Dan Sullivan. It's really powerful in helping everyone identify what matters most. And the best part? It only takes about 10 minutes, depending on the size of your group. Here are the steps:

1. *Ask "What's It Worth" questions and have everyone write down their answers.*
2. *Challenge everyone to write down 3 responses to "What's Worth Doing Every …"*
3. *Invite the group to share some of their answers and watch the magic happen.*

WHAT'S IT WORTH?

Question #1: What's worth keeping track of daily? Answers to this may include everything from tasks on a key project at work, to exercise regimens or nutritional intake on the personal side of life.

Question #2: What's worth always measuring? No, this isn't the amount of flour in a cake, but rather progress toward a company sales goal, or financial asset growth, or on the individual level, maybe personal transformation or spiritual goals.

Question #3: What's worth saving and/or preserving? This can include archiving your company's achievements, whether for annual reviews, or web site case studies. On the family or personal side of life, it can be photos, memories, journals with inspirational thoughts.

Question #4: What's worth investing time, money, and energy in? Answers here often include investing in professional or ongoing education, skill development, company growth, etc. Within our families, it can be things like higher education for children or grandchildren, humanitarian missions, and more.

Question #5: What's worth remembering permanently? For companies, answers here include learning from the lessons of success ... and failure. We can track the things that work well, and even the things that don't to improve company performance and overall success. On an individual level, this can mean recording how we felt on the big moments of life – baby births, baptisms, weddings, funerals, big successes, and even the day-to-day triumphs.

Question #6: What's worth sacrificing for? Within a company, answers here can vary, but usually they focus on coming through for a client, or maintaining company integrity when it may be tempting to take the shortcut. At home, answers often include sacrificing for siblings or parents, country and freedom.

Question #7: What's worth fighting for? This question goes even deeper, and answers often include doing the right thing for the client, maintaining profitability, etc. Again, on the personal side of life, religious freedom, beliefs, and well-being are among the most common responses.

WHAT'S WORTH DOING EVERY ...

Next, ask your team to write down three responses to each of the following:

- *What's worth doing every year and why?*
- *What's worth doing every quarter and why?*
- *What's worth doing every month and why?*
- *What's worth doing every week and why?*
- *What's worth doing every day and why?*

To offer personal examples from my own family's life, every year activities include holding a Family Vacation with a Purpose, to bond and pass along KASH (Knowledge, Attitude, Skills and Habits). Quarterly, my wife and I like to get away for our own couple's retreat and review our goals for the next three months. Every month, my family engages in charitable giving through our church. Every week, my wife and I go on a date to keep our relationship close. And every day, we head to the gym together for running, boxing or strength training.

By having everyone identify answers to these What's Worth Doing Every questions, you'll be able to watch your team identify the most important activities on a big-picture annual basis, all the way down to daily practices.

SHARE THE INSIGHT

Finally wrap up the activity by inviting some of the group to share their responses. Depending on time, you can have everyone share everything, or just the highlights. You'll be amazed at the perspectives you hear, and how everyone can learn from each other.

I like to do the What's It Worth activity at least once a year with my team, as well as with my family. It helps provide clarity and direction, as well as cohesiveness as a group. I challenge you to do the same, and wish you greater understanding, insight and success as you do.

HOW TO AVOID ABSOLUTELY UNACCEPTABLE REGRETS

There are turning points in everyone's life. The education we pursued, the career paths we took versus the ones we didn't, the family and friends we've surrounded ourselves with, and the list goes on and on.

As we look back, we're grateful for the decisions and actions that turned out favorably. Inevitably there are some that weren't so fortuitous, and we may wish we could go back and correct the course. But while the ups and downs of life are normal, what all of us want to avoid are the big mistakes ... the ones Dan Sullivan calls "absolutely unacceptable regrets." Again, I appreciate his brilliance in providing tools that I have then adapted to live an abundant life.

So, here's another powerful exercise you can do with yourself, your children and your grandchildren (if they're at least early teens). It's something I have done with my employees, my wife, my children, and even the Boy Scouts I volunteer with (which was an eye-opening experience to see its impact on 14- and 15-year-old young men).

There are just two rules to this exercise:

1) Be thorough—reach deep to answer the questions as completely and clearly as possible

2) Be honest—all progress begins by telling the truth.

PART 1 - MAKE THE LIST

You start by taking about 10 minutes to answer the following question: At the end of ... (fill in the time-frame — the quarter, year, five years, your career, time on earth, etc.), what are five absolutely unacceptable regrets you would NOT want to have?

Answers may include not making amends with an important person in your life; not taking the time to be with an aging parent or capturing their life story in recorded interviews; not taking care of your nutrition and exercise which could lead to chronic illnesses like diabetes; not achieving family financial goals or taking long-anticipated trips; not starting a business or pursuing a particular career; not developing personal talents; etc.

PART 2 – DELVE DEEPER

Once everyone has identified five absolutely unacceptable regrets, the next step is to answer these questions (apply each question to all five regrets):

- *What would be so unacceptable to you about each of these regrets? (The goal here it get very clear on the specifics of WHY these would be unacceptable.)*
- *What are you doing or not doing right now that might bring about such regrets? (This is the moment where you face the music. Honesty here will be critical.)*
- *By what specific date—at the latest—do you need to make changes to avoid this regret? (Instead of just talking about it, you've got to identify a date that will help you avoid this regret.)*
- *What measurable achievement or result will prove that you won't have this regret? (Here's where you set goals. And remember, make them SMART goals: Specific, Measurable, Attainable, Relevant, within a Time-frame.)*

- *90 days from now, what progress will you report and to whom? (Don't keep this just to yourself—accountability is important whenever we're making changes.)*
- *What is the first action you are going to take? (You've got to get into motion and take that first action immediately—this will help set you up for success.)*

I've seen the power of this exercise time and again. On a personal note, when my wife and I did this for the first time, we thought we'd whip through it in about 20 minutes before dinner. That turned into an hour-and-a-half before dinner, and continued conversation late into the night after dinner. We had been married for thirty-eight years at the time, and this was one of the most intimate, incredible and bonding experiences we'd had to date … a moment I will never forget.

Perhaps it's the honesty. Maybe it's the voicing of the unspoken fears. But when we bring things out of obscurity into the light, amazing things can happen. We realize we are not victims of chance and fate, but that we are empowered to chart our own course toward success. We see that we can avoid the absolutely unacceptable regrets. It just takes honesty, clarity, vision and action. And that's exactly what this exercise helps provide—so you don't run out of gas and get stranded.

Don't waste a minute. Plan now to lead this exercise with yourself and your family. Because clarity and action can take you to important turning points in the road, ones that lead to abundance. And isn't that what you and your family deserve?

ACTING IN HARMONY

A book written well over 110 years ago, titled *The Majesty of Calmness,* was authored by William George Jordan. He also wrote a book called *The Power of Truth.* When you read this book, you'll think that he wrote it yesterday for our time. *The Majesty of Calmness* is one of the favorite books we read as a family on our Family Vacations with a Purpose. It's a short, two-hour read, but very deep and thought-provoking. It is from this book that we designed the theme to consciously train the mind and body to unconsciously act in harmony with our family values and vision.

So, the highlight of any Family Vacation with a Purpose is the day that we do this exercise. I do this exercise with youth at the youth detention center. I've done it with boy scouts around campfires. We do this with our children and grandchildren. I do this with our employees. It is one of the most powerful ways to be sincerely interested in other significant people in your life. This will ensure that they do not run out of fuel when things happen or when they have headwinds or resistance or setbacks in their lives. To consciously train your mind and body to just unconsciously act in harmony with your family values and vision, you must first outline and identify clearly what your family values and vision for a brighter future are. We do this by envisioning a time frame. These are SMART goals. Again, SMART is an acronym that stands for **S**pecific, **M**easurable, **A**ttainable and **R**elevant in a **T**ime frame.

When our family meets in Maui every two years, the time frame for setting goals is two years. So, we ask our children to take 15 minutes and write down—if we were meeting here two years from today, (which we will be), looking back over that two years to today—what has to have happened in your lives for you to be happy with the progress that you made with all of your assets (not just financial assets, but your foundational assets and your intellectual assets).

They go through and fill it out in the three dimensions of Authentic Wealth (foundational, intellectual, and financial). Then, we have them answer, "What are the biggest dangers, roadblocks, hindrances, that would stand in the way" that they need to eliminate. This increases the likelihood they will achieve that vision from about 55% up to over 90%. Then, we have them identify the greatest opportunities that they need to seize in order to do so, and then identify the greatest strengths or resources they're going to harness. This dramatically increases the chances that these things will come to fruition. You will be amazed at how many times people consciously train their mind and body and then they unconsciously align themselves to see it come to fruition. You see, just hoping for something is not enough. You must have faith, but it must be coupled with works. But as you articulate your goals and vision for a brighter future, I am convinced that many of your fondest dreams with help from a Higher Power to bear upon your circumstances will provide opportunities that you did not even recognize before.

Whenever we have done this, every one of our children has achieved what seemed to be nearly impossible within that two-year time frame because we all got on board in an abundance mindset support group to help one another achieve our goals. This exercise is a take-off from the R-Factor and DOS (Relationship Factor and Dangers, Opportunities and Strengths) exercise I shared in Chapter 5. It's visualization on steroids.

I remember one year in Maui, just prior to going around the family circle with our six children and their spouses, wherein they articulated what has to have happened in their life for them to be happy with the progress they made during the next two years. My son-in-law, Scott, suggested that we take a moment and share one thing that we wrote down two years ago and see if it came to fruition. What a great idea! Talk about an amazing payday as a parent!

Going right down the list, our oldest daughter two years earlier had been very frustrated with a setback in her life. She was going through a very difficult divorce and was frustrated because of not being able to move on with her life because of the resistance and lack of responsibility and accountability from her ex-husband. She could not see any light at the end of the tunnel. Miraculously, even though many of the issues had not completely been resolved, there had been tremendous headway accomplished and she was able to feel much better about her brighter future.

Our next child and her husband wanted to get into a new home, but it was a soft market and financing was difficult to obtain. In that time frame, they had located a beautiful dream home, were able to purchase it, move in and their children began to make friends with some incredible young people and they loved their schools and the new neighborhood.

My next child, a son, and his wife had been trying for five years to conceive their own child if possible. They were fine with adopting but really wanted to conceive their own if possible. They expressed that desire and unitedly as a family, we exercised a lot of faith and prayers on their behalf. In a couple of months on Father's Day, they came to our home and announced that miraculously, they had conceived their first child. The product of that was their first little boy named Ethan Douglas. He is so cute they almost moved his middle name up to his first name! Since then they have miraculously conceived two other cute, little darling girls.

Our fourth child, another son, was frustrated in trying to find the girl of his dreams to marry. In that two year timeframe, he found her and they were married with a wonderful family celebration, all of us dressed in white. They were in their new home and expecting their first child.

My fifth child, a daughter, and her husband were embarking their journey to Iowa to attend dental school. They had qualified for an incredible scholarship, were able to purchase a home in the town where he was attending college (rather than rent), and also our daughter was able to secure a very high paying position as an esthetician at a spa. They were able to start their family and incredible things had fallen into place for his experience while in dental school and subsequent residency at the University of Minnesota.

Our last child, a daughter, had been frustrated trying to find a young man that she knew she could be happy with as a marriage partner. She was on a semester abroad in New Zealand when a young man that lived down the street from us and was actually one of our son's best friends, was getting interested in another young lady. She could never imagine herself having a romantic relationship with the boy down the street. But she wrote home and said I'm feeling jealous, what's happening? She came home and was able to realize that she had feelings for this young man. He jumped at the chance and they got engaged and married during that time period, and she realized how special he was to her.

All the way down the line, our six children had accomplished one of the top three things that they had circled as most important to them during that time period. And even though they could not see how it would come to fruition two years earlier, it had all happened. This is the power of consciously training the mind and body to unconsciously act in harmony with your values and your vision.

FLIGHT SCHOOL

Whether it's in business affairs, family life, charitable efforts—every aspect of life, really—we only truly prosper when we grow. And one of the laws of lifetime growth? Always make your learning greater than your experience. As you look at the different aspects of your life, consider how this principle plays out so you can avoid pitfalls and prosper.

We often point to the successes in life as some of our greatest experiences. But Roy and I would like you first to reflect on the negative ones. As indicated in Chapter 4, Walt Disney went broke about seven times and had a nervous breakdown before he finally made his breakthrough. Thomas Edison failed over 16,000 times trying to invent the electric light bulb, but he said, "I haven't failed 16,000 times. I've successfully found 16,000 ways that don't work."

For me personally, some of the greatest breakthroughs I've ever had in my life, or epiphanies, came from the negative experiences. Many great people have learned from their setbacks. Years ago I used to make occasional business trips to North Las Vegas, where my firm had an office. As a licensed pilot, I would often fly there on one of our two planes, a Piper Archer or a little Cessna 152.

One particular trip, I brought my daughter Mailee, who was five years old. We took the Cessna, departing from the Provo Airport to North Las Vegas. Now I had taken this trip dozens of times, and I always arrived with about a quarter-tank of fuel remaining. This day there were headwinds, and I wanted to stay under the clouds so I took a different route—not the usual path as the crow flies—but one that followed the I-15 corridor.

I was halfway between St. George, Utah, and Las Vegas when I looked down at the fuel gauges for the first time. These instruments had been in front of me for over two hours, the needles were buried in the red, and I thought, "How did I not realize that I was flying into a headwind, taking a longer route?"

At this point it wasn't a matter of "would" I run out of fuel; it was "when." I knew I couldn't turn around and go back to St. George. My tank would hit empty over the Virgin River Gorge, and if you've driven through those steep canyons you know that is not a place you'd like to make an emergency landing. I had to keep going. So I kept my altitude at 10,000 feet and kept looking for options, with questions racing through my mind: would I land on I-15 with the traffic ... or maybe in a field with furrows ... how would I avoid telephone poles, etc.?

I've never prayed harder in my life. Finally we were able to see Las Vegas in the distance, but in our path was Nellis Air Force Base—restricted airspace. I called in on the frequency and said, "This is Cessna 5155 Bravo requesting permission to land

and refuel." The man said, "Permission denied." He went on to tell me not only that, but they were doing F16 maneuvers and he demanded I skirt to the north.

I explained my situation and said, "I can't, sir. I'm going to fly through your airspace." He said, "You're going to do so at your own risk." He then told me which frequency to tune into, and he got the F16 pilots to do the same. He talked me through, saying things like, "5155 Bravo, you've got two F16s at two o'clock. Verify. Now you have two at eleven o'clock."

Talk about nerve wracking. I felt like this little moth flying through a bunch of hornets. When I finally got through, I began to approach North Las Vegas. When I saw there was no traffic in the pattern, they gave me permission to do a straight-in. I put on my flaps, came out of the sky, landed and ran out of fuel just as I was taxiing off the runway.

The airplane held 26 gallons in the two wings. The young man who came with the fuel truck put in 28 and-a-half gallons, and he asked, "Do you know how empty you were?" I said "Yeeeesss. Uh, I ran out." I'll never forget; he said, "Man, you like to live on the edge, don't you?"

Well actually I don't, and I was determined to learn from this mistake. I asked myself, "When we have signals right in front of us, why do we ignore that they're warning us of danger?" Needless to say I have never allowed myself to get even close to empty again, and I have applied this principle to other aspects of my life—and taught my children to do the same.

Borrow from my experience and ask yourself which signals you might be ignoring. Are there signs that you need to make changes with your business or career? Are your family relationships on a quarter-tank—or worse—in the red? What about your financial plans? A lot of Americans are oblivious to the fact that we are flying into economic headwinds. Taxes are going up. Inflation is going to erode away the purchasing power of our dollars, and we're going to continue to see market volatility.

While you may not find yourself piloting a plane—or even riding a Harley for that matter—consider what you can do now to prevent running out of gas, or worse, crashing, in all areas of your life. Because I can tell you from personal experience, there's nothing like coming in for a safe landing.

RETHINK YOUR THINKING

U: *How can YOU . . . ?*

- *Be more aware of how much "fuel" you have in your "tank?"*
- *Determine what's worth it?*
- *Avoid absolutely unacceptable regrets in life?*
- *Maintain a "majesty of calmness?"*
- *Consciously train your mind and body to unconsciously act in harmony with your values and vision?*

F: ***How can you empower your close circle of FAMILY and FRIENDS to do the same—by organizing and conducting activities where you can discuss what matters most?***

O: *How can you encourage OTHERS with whom you work and serve to do the same?*

11 SOME OF THOSE BUGS STING

Roy:

It seems that Harley riders are always pictured with bugs stuck between their teeth. We're always smiling, and the bugs you run into seem to hit you right in your front teeth. Riding a Harley and dealing with bugs is part of the adventure. But, I have learned over the years that the bugs are not always a laughing matter. Some of those bugs sting.

My first experience with serious bee stings was when I was moving some old dead logs near our home along the golf course. As I lifted one of the logs, I was attacked by a swarm of angry bees. As fast as I could run was not fast enough, and they were all over me doing their thing. I recovered, but that memory is still in the forefront of my mind.

Several years later, when riding across Colorado on the Harley, a bee hit me in the neck and in went the stinger. My neck swelled up like an old turkey in a matter of a few hours. I thought, "Oh well, stuff just happens."

After that incident, I put "Ape Hanger" handle bars on my bike, which results in your arms riding high and your sleeves being a perfect net to catch bugs. For three straight summer riding seasons, I was lucky enough to be able to catch a bee in that net, and of course the bees obliged by giving me their stinger. This past summer was the most severe reaction I have ever had. My arm swelled up from my elbow down, and my hand joined in the fun.

My wisdom has grown. I now do all I can to avoid the bees by creating a sleeve catcher with a wristband. I also carry an antidote, an EpiPen®, to use just in case of a sting. (I am now very allergic to bee stings.)

Once again, there is a life's lesson to be learned here. Alcoholism has been shown to often be genetic in nature. If you are prone, you might have only one drink and find yourself on a downward spiral, suffering from a life of failure and sorrows. Pornography is available with the click of the mouse, which could get you hooked and destroy your marriage and family. The drug culture is all around us. The crew is always looking for new recruits, not only for financial gain, but because those folks want to increase their social circles.

As a Christian, I believe God wants us to be free from such things. We think we might get just one sting here and there, thinking it's no big deal. But then it can lead to another, and another, and eventually it can be life threatening.

None of us knows which of these stings could be our greatest weakness. What is our defense? First of all, it is prevention. Put on your wrist bands and don't let those buggers get down your sleeve. Second, if you get stung, get help. The truth is, your sensitivity and severity of the allergic reaction grows with each encounter. These things can be life threatening. Until you can put addictions or other harmful things in your life behind you, your progress in this life is dead on the side of the road.

Doug's Take:

Well, thus far, I've never been stung by a bee while riding my Harley. But I do know the feeling of getting hit in the face several times going over 60 miles per hour down the highway—bugs pummel your forehead like a rock.

On one ride, a bee somehow got trapped in my helmet and by the time I pulled over to get it out, Sharee surmised I was having epileptic seizure. On long trips, I always take a few rags and bug remover to not only clean off my windshield, but also my leathers at the end of the day. Of course, nothing makes a Harley rider look more seasoned when he or she struts into a cafe than a "doo rag," sunglass lines, and a large collection of bugs splattered all over their leathers.

In the year 2000, we joined a group of about 30 bikers on a tour from Atlanta, Georgia, down to Key West, Florida, and then back through the Everglades and ending up in Orlando. We ran into one hundred bazillion love bugs. Love bugs are a member of the family of March flies. They are also known as the honeymoon fly, kissingbug or double-headed bug. They are named such because during and after mating, adult pairs remain coupled, even in flight for up to several days. This ride was in May, and during one part of the trip we had to stop about every 20 minutes to clean our windshields, coated in love bugs in that short of time-frame.

So sometimes, not only are bugs dangerous for their sting, but often they can accumulate and impede our vision for a brighter future in life. Sometimes bugs can be removed from our windshield of life with a simple swipe. But most of the time it requires us to stop and wash our windshield clean. Sometimes that cleansing requires strong solvent (which comes from the root "solve") to clear up our problems.

As you are aware, sometime chips happen on our windshields. The best thing to do is repair the chip with resin as soon as possible to prevent it from spreading into a serious crack—requiring a complete replacement of our windshield. Some bugs contain strong acids that if left on the windshield for an extended period, will pit and erode away the smooth clear finish. I think you get the message. It behooves all of us not to wait too long before removing the bugs in our lives—with whatever remedy is needed to get our vision extremely clear and smooth again.

HAPPINESS COMES FROM WITHIN

In my years of presenting to audiences around the world, I have learned there are some common denominators. No matter how diverse the audience—multi-millionaires or youth in boys and girls group homes—there are similarities.

I have discovered that many times, people throughout their lives are searching for happiness through the accumulation of *things*. No matter how many things they acquire, they never seem to be satisfied. Young people will try to be happy with the latest and greatest smart phone or iPad technology, skateboard, bicycle, motorcycle, car, or water skis. Adults often times think they will be happy when they finally have a bigger home, a cabin, a condo, a boat, a motor home, jet skis—whatever it is, they think those things are going to result in, "I will finally be happy when. . ." Many billionaires are very unhappy people as they continually strive for the accumulation of things.

The second thing that people try to find happiness is through other people. Young people many times can't seem to find happiness or satisfaction with their own lives. They are looking externally toward movie stars or athletes, living their lives through others, looking at Twitter and Facebook and wondering what Miley Cyrus or Justin Bieber or some other celebrity is doing.

I find this to be very true with adults also. Many times they focus on movie stars or professional athletes or even personalities on radio and TV. For example, on many of the radio stations where my weekly show is broadcast, other conservative talk show hosts such as Glen Beck, Rush Limbaugh or Sean Hannity are often on the same stations. Make no mistake, I enjoy hearing their viewpoints. But, it is amazing to me how many times I find that people don't want to make any of their own decisions or do their own thinking. They want those people to be the movers and shakers to influence government or politicians. They are living their lives through other personalities.

They are in essence people worshippers, and they have what Dan Sullivan calls "decidephobia," as I introduced in Chapter 7. They do not want to choose their own future; they want somebody else to do it. They don't want to make commitments and find happiness with their own lives. They are always living on borrowed light, rather than their own light. That's why they have a hard time understanding that happiness comes from within while getting great ideas and inspiration from other people.

The problem is usually all we do is get warm and fuzzy feelings of inspiration. When we transform that inspiration to motivation, we are now moving in the right direction. However, it's not until we transform motivation into implementation, that we see an actual change take place. When you implement the principle through proven strategies and concepts utilizing the best tools, a change takes place in your life and you are progressing.

The third area that people try to find happiness is through worshipping thought. In other words, I've often heard people say such little quips as, "If it sounds too good to be true, it probably isn't true." I just snicker, because many things in my life that sounded too good to be true ended up being true. In fact, I often ask audiences, if what you always thought to be true, turned out not to be true, when would you want to know? Or, if what you always thought to be *not* true, turned out *to* be true, when would you want to know? Sooner than later, right?

We all have thoughts that have been ingrained in us because of the way we were raised, or perhaps from people we have hung out with. Often, they've passed on a scarcity mentality. We hear, "There's no such thing as a stupid question!" Well, we should always make our questions bigger than our answers, but that statement just isn't true. I've heard lots of stupid questions in my life. Just listen to some of the call-in shows after an athletic event.

Many times people will latch on to thoughts such as, "Well, you should have unconditional love." This is a term that many Christians have invented, and I have yet to find the term "unconditional love" in any scripture. It could prove to be disastrous depending on how we interpret what that thought means. I have heard interpretations from one end of the spectrum to the other from many people. When I say, "Explain what unconditional love means to you." If they respond, that it means you love everybody regardless, I say, "Okay, that sounds pretty good on the surface, but explain regardless."

Many times people say that unconditional love means you treat all of your children the same. I then say, "Wait a minute. What do you mean by that?" Sharee and I have six children and 14 grandchildren. If we treated them all the same (because they all have their own factory-installed unique personalities and unique abilities), we're probably treating most of them wrong.

People often get a perplexed look on their face. Sometimes, I get a response like, "Regardless of what your children do, you need to treat them all the same and give them the same things." I then say, "Wait a minute, I think that's not teaching responsibility and accountability if you really study whatever your belief is of a Higher Power. For example, if you study the Old Testament and New Testament, God is extremely conditional on how He rewards or blesses His children—us. Blessings are very contingent upon us doing what He asks. We receive blessings predicated on obedience to His laws. There are consequences—both good and bad—for the choices we make."

That is why, as a financial strategist helping people with their estate, the vast majority of trusts I review are set up for equal distribution. Regardless, when people pass away, they usually kill the goose that's laying the golden eggs when they divide it up and give every child an equal portion. There's a saying: "There is nothing more unequal than the equal distribution to unequals."

I don't believe God rewards or distributes blessings unconditionally. He is very conditional based upon one's responsibility and accountability. One of the things I have taken pride in doing is helping people set up equal opportunity trusts with rules of governance, rather than equal distribution. This is a way of living and continues under the successor trustees after we pass on to where every child, grandchild, and heir has equal opportunities, but not necessarily equal distribution. Equal distribution is the common approach that the estate planning industry has taken, because it's the easiest route to take. It all too often results in an entitlement mentality and takes families from "we" to "me." As the title of Chapter 1 of my first best-selling book, *Missed Fortune 101,* reads, "All the Dogs Barking Up the Wrong Tree Doesn't Make it the Right One!"

I have worked my entire career to help people re-think their thinking. We should rethink our thinking, with full regard to where happiness or success really comes from. It's not in things, or other people or even thoughts. Most addictions begin between the ages of 12 and 22. I have observed that most addictions whether it is alcohol, drugs, pornography, sex, shopping or eating, usually comes as a result of people not feeling satisfied or happy from within. They are trying to find that euphoric feeling from satisfying it with external stimuli.

When you learn how to create the happiness from within instead of external stimulus, then the human body is a miraculous creation that will release the natural endorphins and chemicals that will have you feeling "high" about life—that you're winning life instead of losing life. In Chapter 8, I gave you a simple formula to feel as if you're on a win streak rather than a losing streak, the remainder of your life. Try it. It works!

STOP THE BLAME GAME

In our company, we often "gamify" (turn things into games) in order learn a new principle and improve productivity. Let's have you play the role of a business leader for a moment. Ready? Here's the situation: So your sales team didn't meet their 3rd quarter quota. What happened when you called a meeting to review the numbers? Was it Joan's fault because she had surgery and couldn't handle her territory? Was the bad economy to blame, with clients too timid to renew their contracts? Or was the whole team simply despondent, sinking in the quicksand of failure?

Have you noticed it's not necessarily **that** we fail, but **what we do when** we fail that can make all the difference? Dr. Edwards Deming, the renowned 20th century statistician, professor, author, and consultant, taught that people often choose to operate in zones of blame, justification or shame, which he said was an absolute waste of time, energy, and money. He explained that only when we deal above the line, acting with responsibility and accountability; we progress.

But how can you help your employees or your children live above the line, leaving behind the temptation to wallow in blame, shame or justification? Try what I call the "$2 Rule."

Marshall Thurber, successful attorney, businessman, author, public speaker – and one of my mentors – took the advice from Dr. Deming and challenged a Fortune 500 company to use the $2 Rule for 90 days: Any time employees chose to deal below the line, they had to contribute $2 to jars located throughout the office, with the proceeds designated to go to charity. In ninety days, they collected a quarter of a million dollars. A quarter of a million dollars! While this was a great windfall for the charity – the greater result was that the exercise raised the employees' awareness of how often they allowed negativity and blame to permeate their day-to-day work. That heightened awareness brought about change – the company's productivity went through the roof, and eventually everyone got a raise.

I've instituted the $2 Rule not only with my employees, but with my family, as well. We even take it with us on our family vacations with a purpose.

If we were to go scuba diving, for example, and our daughter Mindy showed up without her snorkel mask and fins, what would happen if she used an excuses like, "Well, I would have remembered, but Aaron was bugging me, so I forgot," she'd be blaming, and she'd owe $2 to the jar. "I broke the straps on my fins yesterday snorkeling, so I didn't bring them"? She'd be justifying, and she'd owe $2 to the jar. Or if she said, "You know me, Dad, you always have to remind me," she'd be operating in shame, and $2 would go to the jar. Why? No matter the excuse, the result is the same. We would have to go back and get the snorkel, mask and fins, which like Dr. Deming points out, is an absolute waste of time, energy and money for the entire family.

What would happen if you set up jars and challenged your employees or children to the $2 Rule? True, you might gather enough for a sizable donation to charity, too, but you'd also likely be surprised at how much everyone starts to rally behind choosing accountability and responsibility. When implemented in a positive, fun way, the $2 Rule often becomes contagious, with co-workers or siblings supporting each other in changing the way they handle setbacks and failures. This could cause ripple effect changes throughout the entire company or your family, which could boost your bottom line and positive family accomplishments.

So go ahead, tame the blame game and see what positive dividends the $2 Rule can pay.

BEAR FRUIT

As a Christian, I taught the life of Christ for eight years on a volunteer basis at an Institute of Religion. Hence, I got very acquainted with the four gospels: Matthew, Mark, Luke, and John. One of my favorite verses is in John 15:1-2. It states, "I am the true vine, and my father is the husbandman. Every branch in me that beareth not fruit he taketh away: and every branch that beareth fruit, he purgeth it, that it may bring forth more fruit."

The setting for this was when Christ was about to be crucified the next day. Judas has already left to betray him, and he is speaking to the eleven remaining disciples. He's telling them essentially God has no use for people who do not bear fruit. Bearing fruit means we are out in the world, in motion, adding value, helping others. He then makes it sound like we have two choices:

1) *We can refuse to bear fruit (by not being in motion and adding value in the world) and therefore God has no use for us. (We'll be eliminated).*

2) *If we bear fruit, in other words if we go out in motion adding value, we're not necessarily "home free." It's almost a guarantee that we're going to be purged with trials.*

God causes rain to fall on the just and unjust. Just because we go through trials in life doesn't mean He doesn't love us. In fact, He probably trusts us enough to throw us a curve ball now and then to see how we can handle the challenge, grow, rise above it and come out victorious.

When I work out at a gym and I put on a weight vest or I lift weights, it's so that when I don't have the weights or when I run outside in a wind, I can have the strength to withstand and endure. Much the same, hard times prepare us for things in life. And like Roy said earlier, I believe we are never given a challenge or a problem in life that our Creator is not confident that we cannot overcome. If we have that faith, we'll know that we are going through any experience to learn so that later on we can bear more fruit and lift others up who are going through similar trials. Those others might be our children, our grandchildren, our employees, our clients—the people we serve. So every challenge in life is actually an opportunity. Instead of looking at it like a difficult challenge and pitying ourselves, look at it as an opportunity for growth so that later on you can bear more fruit and lift others up. In order to lift others up or uplift them, you must be on higher ground.

CONQUER FEAR & BUILD CONFIDENCE

One time, Sharee and I were invited to go to La Connor, Washington, to spend a couple of days with a wonderful organization, Pransky and Associates. George and his wife, Linda, Pransky have an incredible Victorian-style office in La Connor, which is about an hour north of Seattle on the Puget Sound, just before reaching the Canada border. La Connor is right by the Skagit Valley where they hold a huge tulip festival every May.

That year, I looked up La Connor and discovered it was voted the most romantic town in America. So of course, I was all for it. When we got there, I discovered it is quaint, serene, and everything they promised it would be. In fact, when we were checking into the little lodge, the clerk asked what brought us to La Connor. We told him we were visiting Pransky and Associates for a couple of days.

This is a small enough community that everybody knows everybody, but this young man was fairly new to the area, and asked, "What goes on over there, anyway?" I said, "Why do you ask?" He told me, "Many celebrities come there, and they think they're incognito because the Paparazzi aren't following them around. They assume we're naive, and that we don't know who they are. But we know who they are. However, when they arrive, they are acting normal—like they do out of the public's eyes, which is usually barking at each other. But within a day after visiting Pransky, they're walking down our streets arm-in-arm, all lovey-dovey. Is it a sex clinic or something?"

I said, "No. "It is a unique organization where they teach you principles of compatibility and forgiveness." So, we invested two days with Pransky and Associates, and it ended up being one of the most incredible experiences in our lives, and we took our children back there.

George Pransky, for the first half of his career as a psychiatrist and psychologist, was always trying to "manufacture" new behavior out of his patients. This is what he was trained to do; to simply treat the symptoms like pouring cold water into a boiling pot of emotions by prescribing Prozac or other sedatives. Soon the emotions would begin boiling again. He then realized that he needed to remove the actual source—the flame that was causing the emotions to boil over. It all changed when he met an automobile mechanic by the name of Syd Banks.

Syd Banks, as an automobile mechanic, one day was crossing the street, and was feeling really down and depressed. A friend said, "Hey, Syd, what's up?" Syd said, "Oh I'm feeling depressed today." His friend, without realizing the impact of his statement said, "Oh, Syd, you're not depressed, you just think you're depressed!" Well Syd went home and thought about it, and thought about it, and thought about it. Let's fast forward. He became the author of some of the most best-selling books on how mind, consciousness, and thought work. He would fill auditoriums full of psychiatrists and psychologists, and you could hear a pin drop for two days as he taught them how the mind really works.

From that point forward, George Pransky changed his approach. It became a "mining" expedition rather than a "manufacturing" expedition. He realized that people's healing comes from within. That they have the power inherent in them, sort of factory-installed. They came with it from their Creator to solve their problems, rather than looking for external chemicals or resources, or blaming their past, or acting out the victim role because they were abused, or the way they were raised.

It's amazing how many married couples have fallen back in love, have forgiven each other, and moved on stronger than ever. It's incredible how many youth—sometimes in less than 72 hours—overcome anorexia or bulimia because of changing their mind, rather than trying to manufacture new behavior.

When George was teaching us, he went up on the board, and wrote down three emotions, not particularly in this order. One was crisis, the other was deadlines, and the other was insults, or offenses. And of course, we all agreed that whenever we experience crisis in life, or we have deadlines looming over us, or if we feel insulted, that we experience anger, stress, anxiety. We get retaliatory, we get upset. He was teaching us that we can do a split second turn—that you can choose to be upset, but you're not obligated to be. And as we began to understand how to do that, I turned to Sharee and exclaimed, "I just got one of the biggest epiphanies of my life."

I've been reading about this in the good book for years. Faith and fear cannot occupy the human heart simultaneously. If I feel fearful, it's a sign I am not exercising faith. Now faith without works is dead. But when I exercise faith and couple that with hard work, the crisis then is no longer stressing me out. I deal with crisis with faith.

When I have a deadline looming over me, such as when the manuscript for my third book was due to my publisher for a $1,000,000 advance in 2007, I can either choose to look at that deadline and get stressed out, or look at it as a lifeline. I can't wait until that date, because it will be the beginning of an incredible future and a book that will become a New York Times and Wall Street Journal best-seller.

When I feel like I have taken offense at something, or been insulted, (as explained in Chapter 6), I realize that most people don't intend to offend, and the small percentage of the time that maybe they did, I just simply forgive, use charity, and realize that they didn't understand what I had been through, or else they would have never said that or judged me that way.

The reality of life is that there are times when we face serious crises, setbacks and challenges. Maybe we get diagnosed with an illness, or we crash our car, or we get laid off. We can get very downhearted, upset, stuck … but remember, we're not obligated to be. It's not to say these things aren't truly tough. But if we exercise faith, the fear will be dispelled. Anytime that I feel fearful, that's a signal I'm not exercising faith. So I teach my children and grandchildren to conquer fear with faith. Because faith puts us in motion, and motion helps us find answers to our problems.

So you can see, the three basic ingredients, faith, hope and charity, can be a powerful recipe for overcoming hard times and finding certainty in an uncertain world. We'll never be immune from crises, deadlines and insults or challenges. But we can change the way we approach them, we can learn from them, and in the process we can lift others to higher ground. And that's a life of abundance, one that is well worth living! I had lived on this planet for 50 years before I really got that.

Dr. Edwards Deming the total quality-management engineer would ask his students, "What takes the time in learning?" After many intellectual replies from students, he would go up to the whiteboard and say, "Here's what takes the time in learning," and then he would write the words: *Not Getting It!*

So Roy and I want our long learning curve for us to turn into a power curve for you. Our objective in writing this book is *getting gotten!*

RETHINK YOUR THINKING

U: *How can YOU ...?*

- *Be better prepared for the "stings" that will inevitably occur in your life?*
- *Be more responsible and accountable for your own happiness and success?*
- *Realize that everyone experiences challenges and setbacks for growth and learning and deal with crisis, deadlines and offenses with more faith, hope and charity?*

F: How can you empower your close circle of FAMILY and FRIENDS to do the same —by being a better example of exercising faith, hope and charity?

O: How can you support and encourage OTHERS with whom you work and serve to do the same?

12 FOLLOWING A TRUCK... YOU ARE BLIND TO DANGERS

Roy:

As I approach the closing chapters of this book, I want to leave you with my belief that as soon as we begin to feel too comfortable in life, we are in danger. We have placed ourselves in a very vulnerable position.

If you have done very much riding in your life, you know that if you pull in on the open road behind a large 18-wheeler and stay on that path, the ride seems very comfortable and smooth. The truck creates a small calm area free of wind and bugs, with no resistance to your forward progression. If you are perceptive, however, you soon become aware that in this zone of comfort there is also a great danger. Your view of the road ahead is completely blocked from view. The truck may straddle a foreign object and then it is, without warning, right in your path. There could be an animal waiting to cross the road ahead, and you have no idea it is there until you are right on it. If you cannot see the face of the truck driver in his or her rearview mirror, then they cannot see you and they have no idea you are there to give you warning should they need to turn or stop.

I will share an experience I had that helped this lesson come to reality for me. My wife and I were traveling a two-lane road in New Zealand with her as my passenger. There had been a very heavy rainstorm the day before. Any earlier attempt to fill the chuck holes in the road were no longer effective. We had been following a large truck for quite some time, waiting for the opportunity to make a safe pass on the narrow road.

We suddenly discovered the truck had straddled a very large chuck hole—but not until we were nearly on top of it! The only option I had was to hold the bars solid and ride through. Some of our gear was thrown off the bike, and my wife was also nearly thrown, too. After pulling to the shoulder to recover, I discovered that both the front and rear rims had been bent with the impact. We were able to regroup and continue to finish the ride on the bent rims, but they both were later replaced at a great expense. This could have all ended much worse with the bike going down or my wife falling off, but once again we were blessed, and lessons like this again made me a wiser rider.

In life, if we feel like we are riding in a comfort zone, and we've got it made, or we feel like this is where we want to live out our days, I feel this is a danger zone. In life, we cannot ride the fence. If we are not pushing ahead into the wind always trying to improve, do better, be a better husband or father or grandfather and servant of our Creator, then we are falling backwards. There is no middle ground.

If we are going to be what we are meant to be, we need to jump into each day and move ahead on our own power. We need to face the headwinds of life with commitment and joy in the opportunity we are given to face challenges. We cannot look for a comfortable spot to ride out of the wind, depending on someone else to make a smooth path for us to ride in. We need to just hit the road's challenges ourselves.

Doug's Take:

Sometimes I have encountered obstacles while riding my Harley that took me by surprise and I had time to miss hitting the obstacle. But sometimes, there has not been time to avoid the debris or a chuck hole. I've had to plow right through it and just hang on—even though on one occasion I also severely damaged my front rim and fender, which luckily was repairable.

Roy and I both are blessed to have cabin properties, each in spectacular settings where we are able to sit and write while viewing a beautiful mountain slope covered with pines and quaking aspen trees. Many times while writing this book I have had deer, elk and moose grazing within view of the picture-window in front of my desk. In fact, a bull moose nearly ran me over the other day while taking a brief break from writing to talk on my cell phone in front of my cabin.

These magnificent animals can be unpredictable. I remember one day while riding back to Salt Lake City in our SUV with my family from a Thanksgiving weekend in St. George, Utah, we encountered a large herd of elk. I could see the elk as they came out of the cedar forest and nervously approached the I-15 freeway. There were a few vehicles that were traveling immediately behind a large 18-wheeler truck—letting it break the path through the slushy, snowy highway. They were oblivious to the herd of elk. All of a sudden, the elk decided to dart across the freeway. The truck swerved and braked, but still hit several elk. Animal body parts and fur flew everywhere. We were fortunate to be at enough of a distance that we could avoid the danger. The vehicles following immediately behind the truck came within a hair's breadth of meeting with fatality. The elk did their normal thing, but unfortunately were not in their natural, safe habitat.

I would concur that the more distance we give ourselves from life's obstacles, the better prepared we can be to handle the challenge. And when challenges come right at us, we need to power through with faith, and repair the damage as best we can.

SOARING TO NEW HEIGHTS

A plane needs three opposing forces to help it overcome the weight or gravity of the aircraft—lift, thrust and drag. Most pilots understand the need to have lift and why the plane's wings are designed to create that lift. It's also easy to understand that thrust is necessary in order to get wind to travel under the flat bottom of the wing faster to create the lift versus the wind traveling over the top of the wing. But what most pilots have a hard time understanding or remembering is the third critical component to getting off the tarmac—drag. You see, if a plane does not experience friction or resistance, it will never get airborne. While in flight, if you lose that friction or drag, it's called a stall and the plane will fall out of the sky—a common cause of airplane crashes.

So it is with our lives, in order to soar to new heights, we must maintain lift in our lives, stay in motion with forward thrust, and it is imperative that we constantly meet life's everyday challenges with gratitude for the friction that keeps us strong. Yes, life can seem like a drag, but not if the "drag" is actually making you stronger and keeping you flying high rather than stalling which will result in crashing and burning.

STAND FOR SOMETHING

An anonymous writer once said, "Stand for something or you'll fall for anything." Oft times, the large trucks that Roy talked about are the people that we get behind in a particular cause or philosophy. As I have explained in this book, many people don't want to make their own decisions or choose their future. They want other people to determine their future. It is based upon seeking for happiness through the accumulation of things or people or thoughts.

Andy Andrews wrote a book in 2013 titled, *How Do You Kill 11 Million People.* It's the story of Adolf Hitler and how he unfortunately killed 11 million Jews, even though there were close to 90 million German citizens that were right there in his country, many of whom thought or knew that something bad was going on. Nonetheless, he pulled off one of the most horrendous feats in history. He points out the German citizens more or less put their heads in the sand in many instances and tried to ignore even some of the signs that there was a Holocaust taking place. Later on, Hitler even admitted how he did it. He said, "If you tell a big enough lie, and you tell it often enough, pretty soon they will believe you."

We have to be very careful getting behind large trucks that can deceive us. Dan Sullivan wrote an essay called the *Fairness Doctrine.* Many times people preach fairness, equality or leveling the playing field, and they usually propose that we need to constantly force redistribution from those who have to those that have not. Historically, it has been proven that the successful people, when left to their own goodness, provide most of the jobs and pay the majority of taxes in America. Yet, when we get too concerned about redistributing or excessively taxing those people, it actually works in reverse and jobs are not created. The companies stop innovating and hiring because every time they do, they are punished. We see continued stagnation in the economy when we create disincentives and penalize productivity.

One of the most dangerous situations historically that civilizations have entered into, is when leaders—be it kings, presidents, rulers or premiers—go about preaching fairness but do it for a hidden agenda. They want to achieve their own unfair advantage, control, or power over their citizens or humanity. These can be the most dangerous leaders, and it is usually not easy to detect their hidden agendas.

We need to not rely on governments to take care of us, but we need to deal above the line, as indicated in the previous chapter and be responsible and accountable. Government is necessary for some regulations and also social services, such as police and safety protection and schools and other public services. But, when we begin to rely too much on government to take care of us in everything we do, we are treading on dangerous ground.

TAKING OWNERSHIP

The secret to American wealth has always been in ownership: deeds, titles and articles of incorporation. You see, when people take ownership, they take better care of things. When was the last time you washed a rental car or changed the oil on a rental car? People don't wash rental cars; they wash their own car! When we own a home, we take better care of it than if we rent a home. That is why for decades in America, we have incentivized people to own. The cheapest money that I can obtain or borrow is to own a home, and in section 163 of the Internal Revenue Code, I can deduct the interest, if I do it correctly, so that it helps me to purchase a home.

We have rights of ownership in America. Countries that do not incentivize their citizens to own, do not have the same standard of living as America. As I mentioned earlier in this book, in countries where the government owns everything, such as North Korea, there is no sense of ownership or the desire to take care of things.

When we take ownership to provide for our own retirement, instead of relying on the government to provide us with Social Security, we do much better. The rate of return on Social Security is one of the worst investments you could ever make. In fact, the government owes over $130 trillion in future Social Security and Medicare benefits, and they have essentially none of that money in their coffers. It is totally dependent on taking from Peter (new workers) to pay Paul (whom they deducted it from before). When we rely on government to take care of us, we then get into heavy debt and dependency.

When we take ownership for our own healthcare, the same is true. It amuses me that we'll spend hours debating the "right" to healthcare, when the real issue is not a right, it is taking responsibility for our health. We all have individual responsibility to take care of ourselves—to be self-reliant. Even if we choose bad habits, poor nutrition or lack of exercise, yes, everyone should have access to healthcare. But we begin to cross a costly line if we insist that the people who choose to be healthy must pay for the people who choose bad habits, and provide them with health care and cures rather than teaching preventative measures.

These are the kinds of difficult discussions that cause nothing more but irritation and animosity between those who are paying (the tax payers) for those who are constantly receiving (the tax eaters). Just recently in the great country of America, the tide has turned to where there are now more tax eaters than there are tax payers. We must seriously look at reversing the direction we're going, rely on fewer government programs, and look more to the citizens being responsible and accountable. The national debt and spending budget in America is out of control.

The concept of taking ownership with responsibility and accountability is not always easy to grasp, because we all want a life of peace and abundance. But how we achieve abundance is by exercising personal freedoms, proper choices and accountability. We can see this throughout the world and in history. Whenever a country has been liberated from communism or even those countries who have been suffering from lack of economic growth because of socialism (where the citizenry bought into larger government and government taking care of them) it is very hard to get them to adapt to being responsible and accountable again. Many times those citizens have become complacent. It's unrealistic to expect a country like Iraq or the Soviet Union to turn into a democracy overnight. Usually, there's a period of mafia and crime that occurs when citizens all of a sudden have freedoms that they did not have before.

In other words, the skills it took the children of Israel to get out of Egypt are not the same skills that it took to get into the Promised Land. They had to wait an entire generation before they could inherit the Promised Land and live a higher law. They were so used to being taken care of with three meals a day as slaves, once they had their freedom, many of them almost yearned to go back and be told what to do so that they could just be taken care of by their masters. We are in serious trouble if we let go of our freedoms and rely on the large trucks in the world to take care of us. It is a precarious spot to be in, and we won't see the oncoming danger until it perhaps is too late to recover.

ENTITLEMENT ABOLITION—EQUAL OPPORTUNITY RATHER THAN EQUAL DISTRIBUTION

Many times we see an entitlement mentality develop among the younger generation. We also witness it with the older generation. It's amazing how fast entitlement mentality happens when we assume we should start receiving something that we've never had before. Often times, when children or families inherit wealth, only three generations pass wherein that wealth is squandered and spent. I know of many people who have had $1 million or $25 million or even $100 million dropped in their lap, and within five to ten years they had absolutely nothing to show for it. In many instances, it has actually been to their demise. It ends up making them turn to addictions in order to achieve happiness or satisfaction because the money did not accomplish that.

The Entitlement Zone is where we just live a life of hope and despair. Many times children of wealthy families grow up born on third base, thinking their whole life that they hit a triple. Many times they don't realize what it took in order for someone in their family, their parents or grandparents, to work hard to accumulate that, and so they feel entitled.

On the positive side is the Responsibility Zone, where you can create predictable results for a brighter future. You take ownership. When I have helped clients with equal opportunity living and trusts, rather than equal distribution, it rewards people and children based upon them having "skin in the game," so to speak.

For example, if a child saves towards college or gets a scholarship, then perhaps you provide a matching contribution or loan. But the loan must be paid back. What if a child wants to go on a humanitarian mission, religious mission or do military service? How about weddings, or for the start of a business venture, or the purchase of a first home? Rather than just constantly bailing children out or dishing money out, it's much better to empower them.

Sharee and I each came from families of six children. We both worked our way through college. As I mentioned earlier, I worked at Kentucky Fried Chicken and my wife worked at a bookstore. I did earn scholarships, as did she. But we worked 25 to 30 hours a week while in school and had excellent study habits because we had to budget our time. By comparison, many of our friends got very poor grades because their parents just constantly shelled out the tuition, fees, room and board.

Hence, Sharee and I, when raising our six children, decided that we would never lead them to believe that we would pay for their college education. We provided equal opportunities. If they got a scholarship or they saved, we would match it—even for a semester abroad, but they had to go abroad to study and get A's—it wasn't just a vacation. If they needed a loan for school, they paid the loan back. If they wanted to start a business venture, or get a higher degree of education and they were short on funds, they had to save towards the project or goal. Then we would match funds, or we would loan them money and they could pay the loan back with a nominal interest rate. We always tried to teach them responsibility and accountability and empower them to make their own decisions. This is part of a very powerful system we call Abundance By Choice where we teach equal opportunity, rather than just entitlement or equal distribution.

UNEMPLOYMENT IS A MENTAL CONDITION

Sometimes the large trucks we get behind that can be dangerous can even be some of our teachers or professors at a school or a university. Richard Rossi, a friend of mine in the Genius Network Mastermind, gave a powerful 10-minute talk on how to prepare children for the future. He gave eight points. I expanded his 8 to 12 things that I feel you must teach your children and grandchildren that unfortunately schools do not effectively teach, and sometimes they're not allowed to teach. In other words, do not sub-contract your child's education to the government.

Many times, young people graduate from college and can't get a job. They think life's unfair; they think the world owes them a living; they become like the Wall Street occupiers. They think the world is evil because they are entitled to a job or somebody giving them a salary or an income. Richard quoted a father who had two children, one got a PhD, the other an MBA. The father had invested $1.5 million on his two children's education, and they moved back home because they could not find a "job."

I strongly believe that unemployment is a mental condition, not a physical condition. You don't go to college to get a job as many kids are led to believe. You go to college to get an education, and unfortunately, many children are not getting much of an education. In our family, we believe in "education" more than "school."

Unfortunately, many of the school systems squash creativity. A test was done where they measured divergent thinking, and they found that kindergarten children scored 98% in divergent thinking—in other words, the ability to see all kinds of possible solutions to a situation. As children went through school, they were tested every few years and their ability to think divergently (which is not the same thing as creativity, even though creativity is an important essential component of divergent thinking), had mostly deteriorated. You would think that it would get better as children got older.

This is beautifully illustrated in a YouTube video called, "Changing Education Paradigms," by Sir Ken Robinson. The main reason for the deterioration is that for years the typical school system has told the students that there's only one answer; it's at the back of the book; and don't look because that's cheating. Now outside school, that's called collaboration.

Children today have all kinds of media and things grabbing their attention and subsequently often get very bored in school. Unfortunately, they are ostracized and diagnosed with ADHD, many of whom may not even really be dealing with the issue. Rather than putting their minds to sleep with drugs, we should be waking them up to the potential they have within themselves. A fellow member of the

Genius Network Mastermind Group, Ed Hollowell, helps ADHD kids "unwrap their gifts," because every one of us has a gift.

The problem is standardized curriculum and standardized testing that often times put our kids in boxes, and they are cranked out of school in batches almost in factory fashion based on their age—or "date of manufacture." Ken Robinson contends that we need to be going in the exact opposite direction in the way we educate.

I devote an entire a day-and-a-half session when I teach these principles to my audiences—usually made up of parents and grandparents. They're not even fully aware that I'm teaching these principles using proven strategies and concepts, including how to implement them with the best tools.

Then I review the list of 12 principles at the end of the instruction, and the audience is always blown away at how powerful and effective these principles are. Below is the summarized list. I have introduced many of these concepts in this book. If you want a more in depth understanding of these principles, you're welcome to visit my website **www.LearningCurvesBook.com** to be able to gain further access to more comprehensive explanations. I'm convinced, if we teach these principles to our children and grandchildren, they will never be unemployed, because unemployment is a mental condition. Security is in the individual, not in a job.

HOW TO PREPARE CHILDREN FOR THE FUTURE

(Adapted and expanded from Richard Rossi's list)

Do not subcontract your child's education to the government. You must teach them the things that schools don't effectively teach:

1. *Critical thinking and problem-solving*
   (How to think strategically, transform experiences into greater learning, and filter opportunities in life)
2. *Conquering fear and building never-ending self-confidence and faith*
   (To deal with crisis, deadlines and insults in life with faith, hope and charity)
3. *Selling, persuading and negotiating skills*

4. *Goal-setting and how to create and maintain a vision for a brighter, bigger future*
   (They should learn to do the R-Factor and DOS exercise at least twice per year for their entire lifetime with regard to several areas/relationships in their lives.)
5. *Effective time-management*
6. *Active listening, effective speaking and articulate writing*
7. *Likeability* (To brighten a room when they enter it; not when they leave it.)
8. *To be entrepreneurial, innovative and self-motivated—what we call "batteries included"* [They should understand and know how to properly use the four entrepreneurial freedoms: 1) Time, 2) Money, 3) Relationships, and 4) Purpose … how to stay in motion and create value for others.]
9. *To consciously train their mind and body to unconsciously act in harmony with their values and vision*
10. *Ability to take negative experiences in life and turn them into positive outcomes*
11. *An attitude of gratitude and an abundance mentality* (versus an entitlement and scarcity mentality)
12. *To always be responsible and accountable* (thereby not dealing in the zones of blame, justification or shame)

Implementing these kinds of strategies in all our lives will help us stay back from the semi-trucks in our lives, making our own safe journey—and enjoying the view along the way.

RETHINK YOUR THINKING

U: *How can YOU ...?*

- *Take more ownership for your own future, rather than relying on others?*
- *Be more of a contributor?*
- *Look for more ways to give and always be in motion, adding value in the world?*

F: ***How can you help facilitate and empower your close circle of FAMILY and FRIENDS to do the same—by teaching them to take ownership for their own success and happiness?***

O: ***How can you support and encourage OTHERS with whom you work and serve to do the same?***

13 ATTITUDE OF GRATITUDE

Roy:

One August, Glenda and I took the opportunity to have a no-plans and no-commitment five days on our Harley in the Grand Tetons and Yellowstone National Park. We always cherish these special times together to enjoy the beauties of our world from the bike's 360° view.

I had, by chance, a special life-changing experience while on this ride. I was somewhat down at the time due to what I, at the time, considered challenges in my life ... and I guess I was just feeling sorry for myself. This was the first week of August, which some of you may know is always Sturgis week. We had decided to not go to Sturgis that year, but I love just being out on the road with all the riders that are coming from or going to that "mecca" of Harley Riders.

We pulled into a view area parking lot to take a rest and had been enjoying this brief break with both feet on the ground when a large group of "real bikers" pulled in alongside us to hang out for a bit. I love the opportunities to hang out with these kinds of folks from all walks of life.

It was not until we were all loading back that I noticed that one of these guys was missing his right arm. I sat on my bike in disbelief as he swung his leg over the seat, grabbed the left grip of his ape hangers and gave the "V-Twin" the starter. He had adapted the throttle from the right grip over to the left. He now had the throttle and the clutch under control of his only arm and hand. He put the bike in gear and made an amazing tight U-turn, the ones I always struggle with, and fell in formation with his group to head down the road. Glenda and I fell in behind their group for several miles as I observed him throttle and clutch with his left hand, shift with his left foot, do all of his breaking with his right foot and ride like the wind.

I left that experience with a new commitment in my life to be able to take what I am given with an attitude of gratitude and be the best I can be at whatever is in my path, with no debate.

My regret from this experience is that I did not have the opportunity to look this "Harley dude" straight in the eyes and tell him how he had been such an influence for good in my life. It is my hope that we might each go forward each day knowing that how we handle challenges in our lives, with strength or with weakness, not only affects our travels, but also the lives and travels of those who look up to us and see us as their mentors.

Keep your rubber side down.

Doug's Take:

Indeed, one of the keys to a happier life is to be grateful for everything in life—the good times and the not so good times. America was largely built on courageous men and women who overcame tremendous challenges to emerge victorious. We all love the story or the movie that depicts the underdog who beats enormous odds, had almost overpowering setbacks, but with perseverance came out on top.

Any successful TV or movie series from *Rocky,* to *Star Wars, Lord of the Rings* and *Harry Potter* depicts countless challenges being overcome. The greatest comebacks in sporting events are the ones we remember the most.

So as we approach each day, week, month and year, let's take note to appreciate (increase the value) the ebbs and flows of life—even into gracefully aging. As we focus on what's going right and what we can learn from experiences—both good and bad—instead of what's going wrong we can avoid the victim mentality, which puts us into the comical but sad conclusion that "Life is hard, and then we die." I implore you to keep living life with zest. Don't go to your grave with your best music still in you. We don't want the epitaph on our grave marker to read, "Born 1960; Died 2025; Buried 2045" because we "retired," or put ourselves out of use, at age 65.

INTERESTING VS. INTERESTED

One of the ways we can appreciate those around us better is to listen. Truly listen. Several years ago a study was done of about 1,000 surgeons. They found that those doctors who spent at least 16 minutes or more being *sincerely* interested in their patients—even if they made a mistake during surgery—the chance of those surgeons being sued was close to zero. However, every minute less than 16 minutes those surgeons spent being *sincerely* interested in their patients the chance of being sued went up about 10%.

At the time the health maintenance organizations were telling the doctors to move on from one patient to the next. One bed to the next. No time for chit chat and visiting with patients. Get down to business and move on. They could not figure out why they were being increasingly sued.

But generally, human beings do not sue other human beings they have relationships with. They do, however, tend to deal below the line in the zone of blame, justification, or shame (as described in Chapter 11) with people they don't have relationships with. This could easily include the doctor, the dentist, the financial advisor, the mortgage banker, if things don't go the way they anticipated.

I used the term "sincerely" a couple of times in the first paragraph above. In ancient Italy when the potters would make pottery out of clay they would put it into a kiln or an oven and when it was taken out of an oven in the form of a pot, many times it would have cracks or imperfections in it. The pottery profession found that if they melted candle wax into the cracks, smooth it over, and paint it, they could still sell the pottery as a functional piece. It would still hold water; but if it ever toppled over, where would it break? Of course it would always break at the weak spot, the crack.

This is where the term "crack pot" comes from. You see, a crack pot is somebody who acts like or has the facade that they have their act together, that they're solid, that they can handle any curveball life throws at them. In reality, they are envious of people who have courage. They often lack gratitude in life. When they have something happen—at the first straw in the wind storm, they fall apart and they crack up and hence they are crack pots.

In the pottery profession if there was a piece of pottery that did not require wax filler—it was solid, or in other words it was genuine, a potter could stamp that piece of pottery "sincere" (pronounced in Italian *sin-chair-reh*) which literally means "without wax." So sincere means that you do not have any "phony" filler.

You've probably discovered that your children can detect pretty quickly whether or not you are sincere—they have little "BS meters." You cannot catch your kids if they're young smoking behind the shed and get after them while you're snuffing out your own cigarette. What you are doing speaks far louder than what you are telling them to do. Many times parents will yell at their kids, "Kids, stop yelling! Stop screaming!" while the kids are seeing their parents doing the exact same thing. They also figure out which parent to go to for things depending upon what it is they want—based on whether they want a parent's permission using emotion (right-brain response) or logic (left-brain response)—but that's a subject for another book.

So, we should make an effort to be sincerely (without wax) interested in others, no matter what "hat" you are wearing at a particular time. In any given month, I wear several different hats, as I am sure you do. Sometimes I'm wearing the hat of husband to my wife, a father to my children, even though they are all adult parents themselves. Sometimes I'm grandpa. I also wear the hat of a business owner, life coach or financial consultant. My wife and I wear the hats of mentors to youth. Sometimes I wear the hat of a Boy Scout leader, or a leader to people in our church, or in our community. There's also my role on my weekly radio show and as a presenter and speaker at many events.

We all look to each other for hope—to see a brighter future lifting them up like a helicopter above the forest. We need that loftier perspective, because we can all get caught up in life and "can't see the forest for the trees." By being sincerely interested in others and listening to them, we can have a powerful impact on those we care about.

WHAT APPRECIATION TRULY MEANS

The word appreciate actually has two different components. When we talk about real estate appreciation, it means that it has an increase in value. When you appreciate people or things or even challenges in life, you're going to experience an increase in value of that thing you are pausing to be grateful for.

The other component of appreciation is to fully understand. When I tell somebody that I appreciate the way they feel, I am attempting to fully understand or empathize with what they are going through. People often reciprocate that appreciation when you've sought to understand them. It behooves us to understand before being understood.

One thing I love to do is write down three to five things or people that I appreciate—and I do this every day. When I do this exercise, it transforms my attitude into gratitude. Try picking at least one person every day or every week to write a simple short hand-written note to, offering gratitude. It is very therapeutic, and it's amazing how many people will respond to that small little gesture of a hand-written note, which is becoming a thing of the past since we have voice mail and e-mail. Try it. You will like it.

But don't stop with yourself. Pass that attitude of gratitude along to your loved ones. While raising our six children, Sharee and I discovered one of the best ways to teach them the principle of gratitude was to share often what we are grateful for. We talk about gratitude for the influence of a greater power in our lives. As explained earlier in this book, we have a tradition of sharing I Remember When memories—little short, real-life stories—that we are grateful for. Often people ask me to give them samples of some of the I Remember When memories I've recorded; so here goes.

WHEN WISDOM KNOCKS, DON'T GIVE IT A BUSY SIGNAL

I have had many experiences in my life where I have had answers to prayers—some which came by virtue of the still small voice; others by small miracles. One of my earliest vivid recollections of receiving an answer to prayer came as a child after our family had returned from a vacation to Disneyland.

Mom and Dad allowed each of the children to buy a souvenir at the corner shop on Main Street Disney before leaving the resort. I picked a little hand-painted, woodcarving bobble-head of Mickey Mouse. My older brother Sherm chose a carving of Goofy. One day shortly after arriving home, Sherm was playing with his Disney souvenir, but I couldn't find my Mickey Mouse. I looked and looked, to no avail. Sherm said to me, "Why don't you pray for help finding it like we have been taught to do?" Even as a child, I felt a little hesitant to bother God with something so "Mickey Mouse." Nonetheless, I humbled myself, knelt down and prayed that I might find it. After praying, I kept kneeling and listened hard with my mind and heart. A distinct voice came into my mind that said, "Look behind the curtain on the window sill!" Sherm asked, "Did you get an answer?" I looked at him and said, "I'm supposed to look behind the curtain on the window sill!" I did, and there was my Mickey Mouse. I knew at that moment and have always remembered, that no matter how trite, if it's important to me, if I pray, He will answer my prayer in His own way and in His own time. That is why I love the parable in Luke 11:5-8 that teaches about importunity.

LOST IN ALASKA

In the late 1980s I had the wonderful opportunity to go on my first hunting and fishing trip to Alaska with my brother Sherm and four other friends. We were dropped off by float plane on a little lake in a remote area of the Ugashick, near the town of King Salmon. It was the first week of October, and the pilot warned us that the weather did not look good. He said if the lake froze during the week we were there, he would not be able to land to pick us up. In that event, we would have to hike with our gear 20 miles to the nearest dirt landing strip.

Well, the next day it stormed; the lake froze; the weather delivered relentless rain and snow; and the wind howled most of the week. In fact, one night the wind blew so hard, it broke our tent poles. There were big brown bears everywhere. I remember how miserable it was, yet what a unique experience I was having. I decided to make the most of the experience regardless of the bad weather.

All six of us were well-equipped, experienced campers. We had all agreed that if we harvested a caribou—and if it were late and we didn't return to camp before dark—that we would not start searching for each other until daylight, because of the surrounding dangers. Hence, we were all equipped with space blankets and survival gear to spend the night solo if needed.

One spectacular evening, I was hiking and came face-to-face with a black wolf. I can still see his yellow eyes. After staring at each other, he trotted off. I sat on a knoll and observed well over 10,000 head of caribou migrating across the tundra—a sight that most people would only see in a *National Geographic* special. I was so enthralled with the beauty of God's creations that I lost track of time. It was dusk when I got up from my perch and started hiking back in what I thought was the right direction. After hiking for a mile or so, nothing looked familiar. I had a strong feeling I was going the wrong direction, and I needed some help beyond my own.

I knelt down and offered a simple prayer for guidance, somehow, some way, to let me know which direction I should go. As I got up and remounted my backpack, I heard three shots being fired. There were no other humans with 20 miles of us. So I knew that it was one of our group, and the shots were coming from the exact opposite direction than where I had been heading. I offered gratitude and promptly headed back. After a mile or two of hiking, I began to recognize the terrain even in the dim night light. Finally I could see the bonfire burning, and made it back well after dark.

When I entered camp, all of the guys stood up and cheered, because they had pretty much resigned themselves to the fact that I was spending the night out with the bears. I immediately asked who fired the shots. It was my friend, my dentist at the time, Garry Brown. I asked, "Why did you fire three shots?" He said, "I don't know really. I just had a strong feeling come over me to get up and sight in my gun. As far as I knew it was right on. But I got up anyway and fired three shots at a target and it was dead on. So I put my rifle back down again and went back to what I was doing."

I can't tell my children enough how much I appreciate our Creator's help in times like these. And they love stories like this. Here's another that has even a deeper message.

AVOID UNACCEPTABLE REGRETS

On Tuesday evening, June 25, 1985 we gathered as a family at Mulboon's Restaurant at Trolley Square (in Salt Lake City) to celebrate our parent's forty-seventh wedding anniversary. It was a lovely evening, and my mother looked dazzling in her gold and white outfit. Two days later on Thursday, I was preparing to open a beautiful new jewelry store in the Layton Hills Mall. The following day was its grand opening. At about 4:00 pm, I closed the electronic gate to the store and was rushing down the escalators to go the parking lot to pick up some critical items in Salt Lake City for the store opening. To my surprise, my mother and father (who lived an hour away) were coming up the escalators. I said, "Mom, Dad, what are you doing here?" They replied, "Oh we were just out for a drive, and wanted to come and see our son's handiwork!" I explained to them that I was in a big hurry to pick up some necessary items for the grand opening. They could tell that I was in a hurry, so they said, "Doug, go! Go and get the things you need; we'll just peer through the gate!" I said I was sorry and darted out to the parking lot.

It was at that moment that the still, small voice said, "Doug, slow down! Spend this time with your mother and father!" It was so clear and distinct that I immediately obeyed and started back up the escalator. Mom and Dad were at the top bidding me to tend to my errands. I refused and instead, opened the gate to the store and showed them around the store, explaining the unique concept with our diamond room. I went next door and bought my mother some Rum Victoria chocolates—her favorite—and we visited while enjoying the delicacies. I never dreamed that would be the last 30 minutes that I would spend with my mother—which I will always cherish.

Two days later while mowing my lawn, Dad called and informed me that Mom had had another heart attack (she had had bypass surgery seven years earlier under the hand of world-renown cardiologist Russell M. Nelson), and that the aneurysm would surely burst and the heart attack would complete later that day. She would pass on. My father invited all of the family to gather at the hospital to bid farewell to our mother late that afternoon. She passed the moment my sister, Patrice, arrived from Seattle. I learned: When wisdom knocks, don't give it a busy signal. Listen to the still small voice and obey! Had I not ... I would have regretted that day the rest of my life.

THE NIGHT MY FATHER HAD ME TURN MYSELF IN

Jobs were scarce when I was in my early and mid-teens. As a young boy I had delivered the Orem *Geneva Times* newspaper, picked cherries for Farley's orchards, and I worked for a while grinding and buffing the metal ears on ski bindings for Miller Ski Company of Orem. On occasion, I would work sun up to sun down in Schofield or Alberta helping brand sheep or building miles of fencing on Cal Jacob's sheep ranch to earn $20 a day.

In 1968, a new Kentucky Fried Chicken franchise was built in Orem, and it paid somewhat better ($1.25 per hour) than McDonald's or the "Hi Spot" hamburger drive-ins where my brother Sherm and sisters, Glenda and Diana, had worked. The problem was, Donald Tuft, the new owner, only needed three chicken cooks at the outset, and more than 150 boys lined up to interview for the job. I was elated when I learned that I was selected for the job, along with two other boys. I was a few months away from 16 years old at the time, and the job required a food-handler's permit which was not normally available until age 16. The county health department made an exception for me, so I took the class and certified. Mr. Tuft told me that I was the only boy that had left him a resume, and on the resume it revealed that I was an Eagle Scout. That impressed him, and he hired me.

I was extremely grateful for the job opportunity and worked very hard to do my best. I held the record for cooking the most pressure cookers of chicken by myself, and was eventually promoted to assistant manager (which meant managing some of my friends who were ahead of me in high school—luckily they were respectful).

One night, some of the chicken cooks informed me that the new diagonal road going from Orem into Provo was finished and opened. It had an overpass road going over it. This was unique because I-15 had not yet been constructed, and overpasses were only to be found on California freeways or on a few train tracks in Lindon and Murray, Utah. They suggested that we hurry and close up KFC that night and go down to the new overpass and toss some eggs at cars as cars went under us. I knew better, but I wanted to be cool with these older schoolmates. So we cleaned up at closing and took thirty eggs with us. We got our kicks tossing them over the overpass at passing cars. To my knowledge, we didn't hit any, but we saw a few brake lights go on.

I got home that evening—no later than I usually arrived—but my mother had intuition like you wouldn't believe. She knew when her boys, Sherm and Doug, were up to "no good." My mother and father were waiting in the living room for me, and as I opened the living room door they asked, "Doug, where have you been?"

I had learned earlier in life that if I lied, I would get into deeper yogurt (so to speak). I felt really stupid as I blurted out, "Uh, I've been down on the new overpass going into Provo throwing eggs at cars!" My confession sounded so idiotic. My father got up from his chair, walked over and put his arm around me and said, "Son, we thought we could trust you!" Wow. They really had trusted me, because they granted me freedoms that a lot of boys didn't have. I had let them down. My father saying that made me feel like a dagger had pierced my chest. Then he said, "Let's go for a ride." I asked, "Where to?" My father said, "To the Orem City Police Department—you're going to turn yourself in."

That was the longest ride ever! About a month earlier, when I closed up KFC the night before the 4th of July (the biggest day of the year for KFC), the store had been burglarized. It was an inside job, because the door was still locked the next morning, and the thieves had hauled out a 300-pound safe full of cash by pouring grease all over the floor. Sergeant Francis Fillmore, one of 27 police officers on Orem's department, called and informed me that the store had been burglarized during the night, but assured me that the owner said I was one of the most impeccably honest young men he had ever met. He just wanted to conduct a routine interview with me and then I could enjoy the holiday (as I was not scheduled to work until 4 pm that day).

Well, I was hoping that Sergeant Francis Fillmore was not on swing shift that night because I was so embarrassed. Who greeted me at 11 pm at the police station? Sergeant Francis Fillmore! He said, "Well, Doug Andrew, what brings you here this hour of the night?" I sheepishly replied, "Well sir, I have a confession to make."

He escorted me into the police station interrogation room where a green lamp was hanging from the ceiling and the fingerprint pads were ready. He said, "Proceed!" I then proceeded to tell him about the egg tossing caper and he let out a big sigh! He thought I had come to confess that I was involved in the burglary! He was totally relieved that I had only been tossing eggs at cars. Then my father asked Sergeant Fillmore to explain to me what could have happened if I would have caused an accident, and I heard phrases like "involuntary manslaughter." I rode home with my dad that night and thanked him for loving me enough to turn me in to the cops. I knew this would be a story I would tell my own children someday—and I have numerous times and to other youth as well. Believe me, I did other stupid things in my youth—but nothing that stupid again!

ALL THREE LEGS ON THE STOOL

We've looked at gratitude, appreciation for others, thanks to God and His help in our lives, and appreciation for life's learning moments. Now let's look a little deeper at those important relationships.

What is your role at work, with employees and clients? Now let's look at home—are you a spouse, parent, aunt/uncle or grandparent? How about church or volunteer efforts, what parts do you play there? What about socially? Are you a member of associations, clubs or friend groups? My guess is your list of roles in life is long, which means you're involved in all types of relationships. Are you making the most of those relationships? Because the more you do, the more successful you'll be in every aspect of your life. As explained, we all find ourselves wearing multiple hats. Each of these relationships matters to me, and I'm grateful for some valuable tools I've learned for building them.

I call it the "three-legged stool" of relationships. It's essentially the foundation of strong relationships, and as you incorporate these, you'll find people are drawn to you—your clients, your customers, your patients, your children, your grandchildren.

The first leg of the three-legged stool is respect. In other words, people don't care about how much you know until they know how much you care, and you have to have mutual respect. Even if their perspective is different, show them you value their position. And as a corollary, people are more concerned about your comfort level with your level of expertise than your actual level of expertise. They want you to be genuine. So don't fake it, be authentic, and truly care about others' needs.

The second leg is rapport. It's developing a connection with those significant people in your life, so they know that you are sincerely interested in them—that it's not just about you. It's about them. Listen to them. Understand them. Walk in their shoes. Develop a bond and uplift them, so that they will feel better about their future or their situation after they interact with you.

The third leg of that stool would be resilience. When we talk about resilience, it's about how fast you can bounce back. This can come into play in several different ways. If you're offering your insight or advice, for example, how do you handle challenges to your counsel? Often when I teach young people or audiences, they will throw curveballs at me on purpose to see how fast I can handle them. They want to see if I'm really genuinely walking the talk. Resilience also comes into play when there are conflicts or challenges in a relationship (which there will be, inevitably). Do you walk away from the relationship, or do you persistently work to understand and resolve the differences? Resilience is critical in all kinds of relationships, so build those bounce-back muscles!

In my 40 years in financial services, while I've helped thousands improve their financial wealth, my greatest joy—and my clients' greatest returns—have come from helping them pursue Authentic Wealth, which includes strong, thriving relationships. I think we can agree when it's all said and done, our relationships will be the thing that defines our lives. So take time to invest in yours. Remember the three-legged stool: respect, rapport and resilience. As you do, you'll lift others, and you'll help them—and yourself—feel confidence in a brighter future.

As we ride down the road of life, one of the things that can help you enjoy the ride the most—and get back up even if you crash—is that attitude of gratitude. It can turn the stormiest of rides into valuable adventures. Make sure to pack it along on all your travels.

RETHINK YOUR THINKING

U: *How can YOU …*

- *Be more "sincerely interested" in others and appreciate them?*
- *Provide an increase in value and fully understand those you care about?*
- *Avoid giving wisdom a busy signal when it knocks*
- *Follow your heart and conscience more?*

F: How can you empower your close circle of FAMILY and FRIENDS to do the same—by helping them be sincerely interested in each other?

O: How can you support and encourage OTHERS with whom you work and serve to do the same?

14 END OF THE ROAD (AN EPILOGUE)

Roy:

The very first chapter of this book stressed that it is not about the destination, but about the journey. Well, there are times on a ride and in life when the entire focus becomes the destination.

I am recalling a group ride we did where there had been a 600-mile day, a 500-mile day and a 400-mile day, all in succession. We had it laid out to arrive just before dark on the 500-mile day, and I had the route planned with a small shortcut I found on the map. We all checked the shortcut on our GPS and agreed it looked good.

After about one hour of riding on the shortcut, the road grew narrower and rougher, and then only continued to get worse. As darkness arrived and I checked the GPS again, a young Native American arrived in his pickup truck to see where we were headed. We soon discovered that about four years earlier, they had abandoned the idea to finish the road. Our only option was to backtrack 90 minutes along our shortcut and then take the normal route.

As we continued the ride well into darkness, my focus was on the destination, not the journey. All I wanted was to bring my wife back safely. As my thoughts turned to her, I couldn't help but think about how I have been blessed in life to always have a wonderful wife along for the ride.

When the destination has seemed unattainable, it has helped to have a hug and a soft shoulder to lean on. During that year after my wife of 48 years passed away, before I was blessed to meet and marry my new wife (and riding partner), I found that without a partner I was without strength, insight, hope and direction.

Yes, life is a journey, and yes man is that he might have joy. But, for me, the joy of the journey is there when man is not alone. I give my thanks for all of those people in my life that have stood by my side, especially when I felt I had reached the "end of the road."

Thank you Frances.

Thank you Glenda.

Thank you family.

Thank you Doug for making this book possible.

Doug's Final Take:

Yes, I do agree with Roy. At the end of the day, it is indeed the destination that we're all striving for, but I believe it will always be an incredible journey, even once we have arrived at that desired destination. The message in this chapter is that shortcuts don't always work out.

One of my favorite motivational speakers early in my career was Zig Ziglar. He used to tell the story about going to the Statue of Liberty in New York or the Washington Monument in Washington, D. C., and how many of the tourists would wait and take tickets to ride the elevator up to the top of the monument. But one day he saw a sign that indicated no waiting for those willing to take the stairs.

Sometimes we think that we want to take the quickest, shortest way to get to the top of our game or the destination, when in reality, life is to be taken one step at a time. There is, in fact, no waiting to get to the top if you're willing to make the effort to take the stairs. Take each meticulous step, and you will arrive.

A wonderful member of the Genius Network Mastermind, Brendan Buchard, is a best-selling author, and he often will ask the questions: "Did I live? Did I love? Did I matter?" I think it behooves us all to ask ourselves those questions. At the end of the day, did you live, did you love, did you matter? What was it all for? Do you want people to talk about how incredible you were and the time that you took for them, that you were sincerely interested in them?

Did you take time to really live your life? Many times, people are so busy making a living, they forget to live. They often don't realize that you have to take time to smell the roses, and make sure those people who mean the most to you know that you love them.

So think about it ... do you really matter? Is the world a better place because of what you do? Are you a giver? Do you contribute more than you receive?

RIGHT PLACE AT THE RIGHT TIME WITH THE RIGHT SPIRIT (RPRTRS)

A principle I teach to my children and grandchildren is to always be in the right place at the right time with the right spirit. It spells an acronym "RPRTRS," which I pronounce REPORTERS. It's because I believe that we will someday all return to God and report on what we did with our lives.

I envision a giant big screen, high-resolution, with the "movie" of our life being played. The nice thing is, we can edit out the parts we don't want played, if we chose to, by repenting of things that we did wrong. If we don't clean them up, we can't sit there and deny that's us upon final release of our movie.

I think it will be far more important to our Creator to report on the kind of husband, wife, father, mother, and human being that we were, than what profession we chose or how much money we made. Our Creator will ask us what we did with the people that He placed in our path. We may at first be surprised and ask, "What people?" I think the first vision that will open up will reveal how many people were brought into our lives for a reason—who were in the right place at the right time with the right spirit, and how they influenced our own lives for the better.

But then a bigger vision will open up, and I'm convinced most people will be blown away by how many people they have influenced—hopefully for the better—by being in the right place at the right time and with the right spirit.

Every once in while I become aware of how this has happened in my own life, yet I was totally oblivious to the fact. One of my fondest memories was the year my Mom and Dad gathered the six children together at Christmas time and asked each of us to think of someone special in our lives. We were going to visit them and deliver homemade fruitcake and goodies.

I chose Rex Blake, my bus driver at Westmore Elementary. He was so nice and drove Bus #2. I'll never forget going as a family to his home on Geneva Road near the Cherry Hill farm. I can still see and smell his living room in my mind. He and his wife were so gracious in receiving our family, and I got to tell him that I had chosen him as my favorite.

Recently in 2013, while attending a funeral for a mutual friend, I met up with Rex Blake, who was ninety-eight years old. His first wife had long passed on, and he married a widow that Sharee knew, Ruth Christiansen. As we visited with them, I mentioned that I would never forget the Christmas that I selected to visit him for Christmas. His eyes got teary and his lip began to quiver, and he shared with me that that year was a very discouraging year for him and his wife. They were feeling really down and having a hard time getting the Christmas spirit. He said, "Doug, you will never know how much that visit impacted us. Your family was really in tune with the Spirit and we were the beneficiaries of your charity." Rex passed away just eighteen days before his 100th birthday, in November of 2014 while I was finishing this book.

UNCLE RICO OR NAPOLEON?

Are you an Uncle Rico or a Napoleon Dynamite? When it comes to how we approach our past, present and future, we have choices in how we handle our progress...or lack thereof. My guess is we'd all prefer to move ahead in life with consistent growth and abundance, but that doesn't happen by chance. We've got to take certain steps, or we'll end up languishing along the way.

It's interesting when I go to high school reunions or similar gatherings how many times people seem to be living their lives in the past. Either they beat themselves up for mistakes that they made 20 or 30 years ago, or they hold on to their accomplishments from yesteryear.

They're looking backward instead of forward, just like Uncle Rico from the breakout film of the early 2000s, *Napoleon Dynamite.* If you've seen it, you'll recall Uncle Rico sitting on the front porch reminiscing about what might have happened if the high school coach would have just put him in during the fourth quarter. He imagines they would have won that football game, and then taken region, and then state. He would have been recruited and gone on to win the NCAA, then he would have made the pros and had a Super Bowl ring on his finger, sitting in a hot tub with his soul mate. Instead he's living out of a van and selling plastic bowls.

Napoleon Dynamite, on the other hand, looks ahead to the future. Despite his current challenges, he goes after what he wants, supports his friends along the way, and in the end finds the love he was looking for.

Which character do you find yourself resembling? And how will that play out in your future? Strategic Coach Dan Sullivan talks about how to determine a brighter future with an exercise he calls the Quick Thinker. You simply take about one or two minutes and you identify the future you want, jotting down about three or four bullet points. Next you decide which part of the past gets to come along--leaving the rest behind. Finally you utilize the present to make the best possible progress.

When I did the exercise, for my future I outlined that I want:

- *Strong family relationships*
- *All of our family's relationship with God to continue to grow*
- *My wife, Sharee, and I to stay in top physical shape and maintain good nutritional habits*
- *To continue to teach and empower my family and others to live abundantly in business, church, community, etc.*

From my past, I decided I want the following to come along:

- *All of our incredible traditions and heritage we've established as a family*
- *The well-oiled machine of predictable results that our company helps provide*
- *The experiences, both good and bad, that we have learned from and that have shaped our future*

I'm going to utilize the present to make the best possible progress by continuing to:

- *Focus on what's going right, not what's going wrong in my life*
- *Have constant gratitude*
- *Always stay in motion and add value to the world*
- *Use the best tools possible so that we can adhere to true principles, employ proven strategies and concepts, and grow in an exponential fashion*

This exercise is relatively simple, but it's been powerful in helping me clarify where I've been, where I am, and where I want to go. I urge you to do the same and start claiming a better tomorrow by outlining what you want your future to look like. Decide which part of the past gets to come along. Utilize the present to make the best possible progress toward a brighter, amazing future. And if you repeat this process on a continual basis, you'll move forward toward a life of abundance. Because like Napoleon, your story deserves to have a happy ending.

TWO OF MY FAVORITE LUNCH BUDDIES ... NOW GONE

A while after my mother passed away, my dad was experiencing severe loneliness. He found a wonderful new companion, Mary Deane, who had lost two previous husbands, one to leukemia and another to a severe stroke. They enjoyed seventeen wonderful years together in the twilight of their lives. One day Mary Deane told me that my brother Sherm and I had given our dad a new lease on life—that we had literally extended our father's life.

As busy as I was in the early 1990s—living an hour's drive from my parents and my brother Sherm—working in my business and raising our six children, I realized I needed to slow down and spend some time with the people that mattered the most. I told Sherm that we needed to set aside a Friday with our dad at least once a month—taking him to lunch and visiting for the day. He enthusiastically agreed. It was sort of like the inspiration I later got when I read the book, *Tuesdays with Morrie,* published in 1997.

We went to our father's home and on his pantry calendar we circled the Friday each month that we would spend the day with him. The anticipation of seeing his two boys every month gave him an incredible renewal. You see, a few years earlier my father had been falling a lot, breaking bones. Finally they performed surgery, but the nerve was not regenerating, and the orthopedic surgeon and neurologist encouraged our dad to just give in to a wheelchair. He refused for more than fifteen years and only gave in during the final months of his life.

Mary Deane said that some months my father would be flat in bed, but in anticipation of spending the day with his two boys, he would muster up energy and strength. He wanted to greet us when we arrived at his door on the appointed morning, dressed in his white cardigan sweater, ready to go spend the day with us. He did not want to be a burden. He learned to use a walker and lock his knees with each step so he could be under his own power. It was remarkable to see him navigate.

We had some awesome experiences traveling around, reminiscing and "Remembering When." I quickly realized that these were golden moments, and that we needed to capture them on a recorder or movie camera. Sherm and I began to jog his memory with different questions, and we recorded his stories and memories. On one occasion, we invited a professional camera crew to come to my office, and we had dad sit and answer questions that were popped at him from his grandchildren. We heard stories we had never heard before! Our children asked their grandpa questions I had never dared to ask.

My dad wasn't a writer. When I was gone for two years serving as a missionary in Korea from 1971 – 1973, I don't recall receiving any "letters" from dad. The letters came from Mom. But I came home from Korea with about 104 cassette tapes—from my father. He knew how to talk. So one year, Sharee and I invited Dad and Mary

Deane to Maui for the week so I could capture his life sketch. I "trapped" him in a room and promised him we would go out to dinner at a fantastic restaurant every night, provided he answered the memory jogging questions I gave him for the day.

I had divided his life into seven segments:

1) *Ancestry*

2) *Early childhood*

3) *Courtship years*

4) *Early married life and child-rearing*

5) *Empty-nester stage*

6) *Church service*

7) *Professional and community service*

I simply asked him to read into a recorder the question and then just talk about the answer. (I told him that if he felt so inclined, he could write some of his responses and just let the pen flow. Well, he never stopped after that. When he passed away I inherited boxes of daily journals that he kept thereafter!)

The point is, in one week we captured 130 pages of his life sketch, then added photos and published his book, titled, *Glenn Andrew, A Man of Steel*—because he was a superintendent at US Steel Geneva works during his career. This book, both published and in digital form, combined with video and audio from our many interviews, were burned on hundreds of CDs and DVDs for about 34 cents in replication costs. We distributed them to family and friends at his funeral. That was more valuable than if every child and grandchild had inherited a quarter of a million dollars! But if we had not captured those experiences, stories and wisdom, they would have gone to his grave with him. Now they will live on forever, benefiting his posterity.

But here is the real message I want to convey. There were many of those Fridays that I had a lot going on in my own life. I was extremely busy—as was Sherm. I would start toward Provo on the designated Friday to spend the day with Sherm and Dad, and as soon as I got halfway there, where my mobile phone could get reception, I would call Dad. He would answer and immediately say, "Is that you Doug? Are you calling to take a rain check? I'll understand; I know how busy you are!" I would always assure him that no, even though I was busy, I had arranged my day to be with him and Sherm.

Sherm and I were fortunate to log over 100 of those Friday lunches with our dad before March 10, 1999. On that date in the evening, the phone rang about 11:45 pm (which is usually not a good sign when someone is calling that late). On the other end was Sue, Sherm's wife, sobbing. The Highway Patrol and just left her home informing her that Sherm has been killed in a one-car rollover while traveling on a business trip toward Nevada. I couldn't believe it. I comforted Sue the best I could, and immediately Sharee and I drove to Sherm's home. I reassured Sue that she would be fine, because Sherm had done what I recommended and he had his financial house in order to take care of his loved ones should something like this ever occur. I wanted to devote the next few days to "celebrating Sherm's life"—his great accomplishments and the kind of man that he was.

You see, he had charisma like you wouldn't believe. He could make a friend out of a total stranger in a movie line or grocery store in less than sixty seconds. He has often been in the right place at the right time with the right spirit for not only me, but many, many other people. And doggone it, he got to "graduate" before me and even Dad! I thought that Sherm and I would be riding motorcycles late into the twilight of our lives, and continue on many more river-running expeditions and family vacations together.

Dad and I were fortunate to enjoy about another 50 Friday lunches together before he passed on in 2005. The point is, two of my favorite lunch buddies are now gone. I will never regret taking time to be with Sherm and Dad. But I also have two lunch buddies in my two sons and now three sons-in-law, and four with my daughters and two daughters-in-law, and at this point fourteen lunch-buddy grandchildren. Most important, I still have my beautiful wife, Sharee, whom I have not stopped dating now for more than 45 years. We go to lunch an average of twice a week. We make sure that Friday night is our date night. If date night gets preempted with something, we always make it up another day. We go on a little overnighter at least once a month.

The point is, if we don't invest time with the people who matter most in our lives, we may end up with absolutely unacceptable regrets. I don't want any of those at the end of the road. So if wisdom is knocking right now, please don't give it a busy signal!

Thanks, Roy, for being the kind of new brother—motorcycle buddy—that I know Sherm would love for me to have until we all rendezvous once again.

I wish you all the best as you make your ride down the road of life. May it be filled with hope, safety, appreciation, love and joy.

RETHINK YOUR THINKING

U: ***How can YOU regularly ask yourself: Did I live? Did I love? Did I matter? Have I seized every moment to be in the Right Place at the Right Time with the Right Spirit?***

F: ***How can you empower your close circle of FAMILY and FRIENDS to ask themselves the same questions on a regular basis?***

O: ***How can you encourage OTHERS at work or in community, church and other social groups to ask themselves the same questions consistently?***

BIOGRAPHIES

DR. ROY A. HAMMOND

DDS, Founder Learning Curves

To say he's an acclaimed dentist and industry leader who went above and beyond for his clients and colleagues ... is just part of the story. To say he's a seasoned rider who has toured the world on his Harley ... would be an understatement. To tell you how he went from taking one humanitarian trip to becoming the founder of his own non-profit and advocate for third-world health ... would give you just a glimpse of his generosity. To say he's a dedicated husband, father and grandfather ... is again but an excerpt of a much longer tale.

Roy Hammond is all these things and more. And he's just added to his resume – author. As an earnest student of life, he shares here a collection of inspiration and insights garnered over his several decades behind the handlebars. And our own journey is all the better for it.

Q: How did you start riding – and how did this lead to your non-profit, Learning Curves?

RH: I started riding motorcycles when I was 14 years old. We lived near the mountains, and I could sneak out the backyard and head up into the hills even though I didn't have a license (much to my mother's dismay). After I finished dental school, I was in a position to buy a Harley Davidson, and I have averaged 10,000 miles a year on the Harley since.

As my wife and I anticipated my retiring from my private dental practice, we brainstormed ideas on how to combine our love for riding Harley Davidsons with the humanitarian work we had begun to enjoy. The result was Learning Curves—dentists come in from all over the world to join Harley tours. Their tuition covers meals, bikes, lodging and continuing education, and the profits all go toward medical equipment and supplies we take on humanitarian trips with groups like Esperanza, CHOICE Humanitarian and Smiles for Life Foundation.

I've been blessed to have two wonderful women by my side (my wife of 48 years, Frances, and Glenda, who I have been blessed to have as my wife for now six years), helping me with the humanitarian work and the efforts to lead the Learning Curves Tours. And we've since been able to share these trips and experiences with our children and grandchildren, which means the world to me.

Q: What do you hope readers will experience with this book?

RH: My most creative moments in my life are when I'm on the back of a Harley, surrounded by the beauties we live in. I go to the lessons I've learned in life. So whether someone is a motorcycle rider or not, my hope is people can pick up these experiences from our lives and adapt them to their own. The biggest lesson? No matter how hard we fall or how long the road we take, there's always a way back, and there's always joy around the next curve!

For more information on Roy's professional background and Learning Curves foundation, visit ***www.LearningCurvesBook.com****. You can also catch glimpses of his great rides there, as well!*

DOUGLAS ANDREW

Founder of Live Abundant

More than 40 years ago, Doug Andrew established his financial practice and quickly established a reputation as a trusted financial strategist. A few years later, Doug and his wife, Sharee, experienced a "defining moment," an unexpected financial setback that changed the way they not only handled their own finances, but also the advice Doug gave to his clients. He adamantly refused to "follow the crowd" and instead delved into extensive research to develop his unique and powerful financial philosophy of liquidity, safety, and rate of return.

In an effort to share his experiences and lessons learned to a broader audience, he wrote his original book, *Missed Fortune.* Doug was thrust on the national stage with the *Missed Fortune book* series that followed, including *Missed Fortune 101* (business best-seller), The Last *Chance Millionaire* (New York Times best-seller and Wall Street Journal #1), and *Millionaire by Thirty* (written with his two sons Emron and Aaron). He is a national radio host and has appeared on PBS, Fox Business, and CBS. He is also a nationally sought-after speaker and has presented for organizations such as Tony Robbins and the Asset Protection Group.

Today he is surrounded by a team of expert financial strategists, Wealth Architects who join Doug in his mission to help clients live an abundant life. They have helped thousands of people not only prepare for and live a prosperous retirement, but also to focus on all aspects of Authentic Wealth—foundational, intellectual and financial assets. And for Doug, who is as passionate about his family as he is helping others realize their abundant potential, life couldn't be better. He has been thrilled to co-author this book with his brother-in-law, Dr. Roy Hammond and share yet another dimension of his life with the world.

Q: What do you find fulfilling about what you do?

DA: I love to share strategies and concepts that transform lives. What gives me energy, what makes me go like an Energizer bunny, is when I see light bulbs going "on"—when I see people realizing that Authentic Wealth is what it's all about. I could do this until my dying day at age 125, helping people see a brighter future by teaching true principles and sharing what mentors have shared with me. I hope this book helps those "aha" moments happen for many people—its insights come from our hearts, our lives, our mistakes and our breakthroughs.

Q: What fuels your personal life?

DA: I absolutely love family. Sharee and I love to spend time together—date nights, lunch a couple days a week, weekend getaways, trips to Hawaii or New Zealand and even exercising. We also love being with our kids and grandkids. We all get together regularly; we have Family Vacations with a Purpose; and we even have Grandpa's Treehouse (a luxury treehouse with air conditioning, swings, and nonstop fun). I share many of our experiences in this book—which makes the book all the more meaningful for me.

For more background on Doug and his work helping others achieve Authentic Wealth, visit ***www.LearningCurvesBook.com***.